INSIDIOUS SOCIAL MEDIA

The Battle for a Generation's Souls

INSIDIOUS SOCIAL MEDIA
The Battle for a Generation's Souls

Myron A. Raney, Ph.D.

Insidious Social Media: The Battle for a Generation's Souls
by Myron A. Raney, Ph.D.

© 2025 Myron A. Raney, Ph.D.

All rights reserved. No portion of this book may be reproduced, stored in a retrieval system, or transmitted in any form or by any means—electronic, mechanical, photocopy, recording, scanning, or other—except for brief quotations in critical reviews or articles, without the prior written permission of the publisher.

Published by Kabalo Life Publishing, an imprint of Kabalo Research, Inc., Columbus, Ohio.

Scripture quotations taken from The Holy Bible, New International Version®, NIV®. Copyright © 1973, 1978, 1984, 2011 by Biblica, Inc. Used with permission of Zondervan. All rights reserved worldwide. www.zondervan.com.

Any email or internet address, phone number, company or product inform, or reference locations printed in this book are offered as a resource and are not intended in any way to be or to imply an endorsement by the publisher or the author, nor do they vouch for the existence, content, or services associated with said email or internet address, phone number, company or product inform, or reference locations beyond the publication date and life of this book.

ISBN: 979-8-218-78424-9
Library of Congress Control Number: 2025940722

Printed in the United States of America

Author Contact: mraney@kabalo.cc

Cover Design by : Markee Books
Interior Design by : Markee Books

ACKNOWLEDGMENTS

First and foremost, I give glory to my Lord and Savior, Jesus Christ. Every word on these pages, every insight and statistic, every story of hope and redemption exists only because of His grace and wisdom. Without His light guiding me, this work would be meaningless.

To my wife — your love, encouragement, and prayers have been the steady heartbeat behind this book. You have reminded me daily that authentic connection begins at home. Thank you for your patience during late nights of research, long writing sessions, and the many conversations that shaped these chapters.

To my mentors, colleagues, and fellow believers who have walked alongside me through decades of ministry, research, and academia — your wisdom has sharpened my perspective and strengthened my faith. Special thanks to those who are affiliated with, and are a part of, the Kabalo Research community who share my passion for equipping communities with biblically grounded, research-driven solutions. Your expertise and partnership continually remind me that the body of Christ thrives through collaboration.

I am deeply grateful for the countless teens, parents, and church leaders whose stories, struggles, and victories gave life to these pages. Some of your experiences are reflected here — always with care and prayer that others might find freedom through your honesty. Your willingness to be vulnerable has illuminated the path toward healing for many.

To the pastors, youth leaders, counselors, and educators who tirelessly labor to shepherd the next generation: your work matters more than words can express.

It has been my privilege to learn from your example and to provide tools that I pray will strengthen your ministries.

To my friends and peers in faith-based mental health advocacy, counseling, and coaching: your commitment to blending compassion with academic rigor has inspired this project's depth. You've proven that scholarship and the Spirit are not at odds but are powerful allies in addressing the challenges of our time.

Finally, to every reader — teen or parent, leader or seeker — thank you for entrusting me with your attention and your heart. My prayer is that what you have read here does not end with information but begins with transformation. May this book be a spark that ignites deeper fellowship, renewed faith, and lasting freedom in Christ.

To God alone be the glory.

CONTENTS

Acknowledgments	VII
Preface	1

The Battle for a Generation's Souls — 5
- Hannah's Silent Struggle — 5
- The Friend Left Behind — 6
- The Harsh Reality of Social Media — 7
- The Outcasts Christ Redeemed — 8
- Understanding Human Nature: Body, Soul, and Spirit — 8
- Light Versus Darkness — 11
- The Battle for the Soul — 12
- The Hope of Christ — 13

The Darkness Behind the Screen — 15
- God's Truth About Light and Darkness — 15
- What Is Really Happening Behind the Screens — 17
- Teen Story: The Trap of Pornography — 19
- A Biblical Parallel: Amnon and Tamar — 20
- The Reality of Devastation — 21
- The Word as Our Guide — 22
- Chapter 1 Reflection — 22

The Seven Deadly Sins in the Digital Age — 25
- The Wages of Sin Is Death — 25
- Pride: The Performance of Self — 26
- Envy: The Poison of Comparison — 27
- Wrath: The Violence of Words — 28
- Sloth: The Idleness of Endless Scrolling — 29
- Greed: The Hunger for More — 30
- Lust: The Corruption of Desire — 31
- Gluttony: The Overconsumption of Content — 32
- Christ, the Freedom from Sin — 32

Chapter 2 Reflection 33

The Ten Commandments and the Battle for the Soul 35
Sinai and the Gift of the Law 38
Love Fulfills the Law 39
"You Shall Have No Other Gods Before Me" 39
"You Shall Not Make for Yourself an Image" 40
"You Shall Not Misuse the Name of the Lord" 41
"Remember the Sabbath Day" 42
"Honor Your Father and Your Mother" 42
"You Shall Not Murder" 43
"You Shall Not Commit Adultery" 43
"You Shall Not Steal" 44
"You Shall Not Give False Testimony" 45
"You Shall Not Covet" 45
Chapter 3 Reflection 46

Addiction, Deviance, and Spiritual Warfare 49
Addiction as Enslavement 49
Deviant Behavior Defined 51
Deviance as Spiritual Warfare 52
The Cost of Body, Soul, and Spirit 53
Victory in the Armor of God 54
Chapter 4 Reflection 55

Boundaries and Spiritual Reset 57
The Need for Boundaries 57
The Call to Spiritual Reset 59
Body, Soul, and Spirit Restored 61
Toward Genuine Relationships 62
Chapter 5 Reflection 63

The Digital Addiction Self-Assessment and Spiritual Reset 65
The Digital Addiction Self-Assessment 66

Beyond the Numbers: Qualitative Reflection 70
The Spiritual Dimension of Digital Addiction 70
Rewiring Neural Pathways 71
From Assessment to Action 72
Spiritual Reset After the Assessment 73
Strategies for Breaking Digital Strongholds 75
Addiction's Toll on Body, Soul, and Spirit 79
The Importance of Boundaries 81
Spiritual Reset After the Assessment 82
Chapter 6 Reflection 82

Breaking Free: The Power of Confession and Accountability 85
The Power of Confession 85
The Gift of Accountability 87
Renewal of the Mind 88
Mental Health in the Digital Age 90
Body, Soul, and Spirit Renewal 91
Biblical Parallels of Renewal 92
A Story of Renewal 93
Chapter 7 Reflection 94

Renewing the Mind Through God's Word 95
The Pattern of This World 95
The Battlefield of the Mind 97
Walking in the Spirit 98
Renewal of the Mind Through Scripture 99
Body, Soul, and Spirit in Renewal 100
Biblical and Modern Parallels 102
The Enemy's Tactics and God's Victory 102
Chapter 8 Reflection 103

The 40-Day Social Media Freedom Plan 105
The Significance of Forty 105
A Spiritual Detox 106
Accepting the Challenge 107

- Days 1–10: Awakening the Soul 108
- Days 21–30: Rebuilding Habits 128
- Days 31–40: Living in Freedom 138
- Conclusion of the 40-Day Social Media Freedom Plan 147

Restoring Authentic Relationships and Family Connections 149
- Authentic Relationships in a Superficial Age 149
- The Family as God's Design for Connection 151
- Body, Soul, and Spirit in Relationships 153
- The Church as a Restoring Community 154
- Reflection 155

Rebuilding Biblical Community in a Digital World 157
- The Nature of True Community 158
- The Call to Fellowship 159
- Community as a Safeguard Against Sin 160
- Body, Soul, and Spirit in Community 161
- Practical Paths to Rebuild Biblical Community 162
- Chapter 11 Reflection 163

The Role of the Church in a Digital World 165
- The Church as a Place of Healing 166
- The Church as a Place of Discipleship 166
- The Church as a Place of Community 167
- The Early Church as Our Model 168
- Body, Soul, and Spirit in Community 171
- Chapter 12 Reflection 171

A Generation Redeemed – Final Charge 173
- The Call to a Redeemed Generation 173
- From Darkness to Light 174
- The Role of Parents and Leaders 175
- Body, Soul, and Spirit of a Redeemed Generation 176
- A Final Charge 177

Chapter 13 Reflection	179

Walking in the Light — 181
From Darkness to Light	182
The Nature of Sin and the Power of Grace	182
The Law of God and the Call of Christ	183
The War for the Soul	183
Boundaries, Renewal, and Reset	184
The Freedom of Confession and Accountability	184
The Practice of Renewal Through the Word	185
A Journey of Freedom	185
Restoring Relationships and Community	185
A Final Charge for a Redeemed Generation	186
A Benediction of Hope	186

Choosing God Over the Scroll — 189

References Cited — 191

Small Group Resources — 195
Foreword to Study Resources	195
Teen Small Group Participant Guide	196
Week 1 – Light vs. Darkness	197
Week 2 – Facing the Battle Within	199
Week 3 – God's Commandments and the Soul	201
Week 4 – Addiction and Spiritual Warfare	202
Week 5 – Boundaries and Spiritual Reset	203
Week 6 – Confession and Accountability	204
Week 7 – Renewing the Mind	205

Small Group Leader's Guide — 209
Eight-Week Curriculum for Teens	209
Small Group Leader's Training	219

About The Author — 221

PREFACE

The digital age has given us tools yielding remarkable power—tools that connect us, inform us, and entertain us. Yet behind the glow of every screen lies a deeper struggle. For today's teens and families, social media has become both a blessing and a battleground. It is a space where relationships can grow but also where souls can be lost.

As an Interdisciplinary Researcher, Board Certified Mental Health Coach and Pastoral Counselor, I have not only studied the evidence but witnessed the consequences firsthand. I have seen the insidious nature of social media that consumes young lives with devastating effects. I have counseled families torn apart by comparison, envy, addiction, and secret sin that took root behind the screen. I have spoken with teens who once brimmed with hope and creativity but who now wrestle with depression, fear, and shame because their value became tied to the fleeting approval of likes and followers. These are not rare or isolated tragedies. They are daily realities in our homes, schools, and churches.

Research confirms what many parents and church leaders already sense in their spirits. According to a 2022 Pew Research Center survey, more than one-third of American teens report being online "almost constantly," with the majority admitting that social media often leaves them feeling worse rather than better. The Centers for Disease Control and Prevention reported in 2023 that nearly 60 percent of teen girls experienced persistent feelings of sadness or hopelessness, the highest level ever recorded, and social media use was a major contributing factor.

The American Psychological Association has likewise documented that heavy use of platforms like Instagram and TikTok is strongly associated with increased rates of depression, anxiety, and sleep disruption among adolescents. These patterns do not simply affect moods — they shape behaviors. Studies show that social media use correlates with higher rates of deviant behavior, including bullying, risky sexual behavior, and substance abuse, as teens imitate what is celebrated in their online worlds

It is because of this devastating reality that I chose to fill these pages with Scripture. The world offers countless solutions — some technical, some psychological, some legal — but none of them can reach the deepest need of the human soul. Only God's Word penetrates both the mind and the heart with transforming power. As Paul declared to Timothy,

> *"All Scripture is God-breathed and is useful for teaching, rebuking, correcting and training in righteousness, so that the servant of God may be thoroughly equipped for every good work."*
> ***2 Timothy 3:16–17***

Scripture is not an accessory in this book; it is the very foundation. Faith-based solutions are not optional for the Church — they are essential, because the battle we are fighting is not merely social or psychological. It is spiritual. As the apostle Paul reminds us,

> *"For our struggle is not against flesh and blood, but against the rulers, against the authorities,*

> *against the powers of this dark world and against the spiritual forces of evil in the heavenly realms."*
> ***Ephesians 6:12***

I have already been asked by many if I intend to make this book available as an eBook, the answer is flat out no! Yes, I understand that today's generation prefers to scroll through pages rather than flip through them. I am well aware that there is a fortune to be made selling eBooks, but the truth is we need not be tempted to redirect attention from the content of this book to scrolling through our social media—we need to pick up a book, not a phone, tablet, kindle, or laptop.

My prayer is that these pages will serve as a guide, a warning, and a source of encouragement. Whether you are a teenager, a parent, or a church leader, may you find in these chapters the courage to set boundaries, the wisdom to walk in truth, and the hope to live free. Above all, may this book remind you that we are not powerless in this battle. The Light has already overcome the darkness, and victory is assured in Jesus Christ.

INTRODUCTION
THE BATTLE FOR A GENERATION'S SOULS

Hannah's Silent Struggle

Late at night, the house is quiet. A teenage girl lies in her room, scrolling on her phone, her face illuminated only by its glow. Her parents believe she is asleep, safe in the comfort of her bed. Instead, she is reading words that cut deeply: "You're so ugly." "Nobody likes you." "Why don't you just disappear?"

Hannah felt invisible. The friends she once trusted seemed distant, her online posts ignored or mocked. Each cruel comment whispered a louder lie — that she was unliked, unloved, and unwanted. She tried to brush them off at first, hoping the insults would fade. When they didn't, she fought back with words of her own, but the response was only harsher, meaner, more relentless. Every notification became another stone placed upon her chest. By the time the night was over, Hannah believed she had no escape. The next morning, her best friend received a message that would change his life forever. Hannah was gone. She had taken her own life, believing the world no longer had a place for her.

The Friend Left Behind

The shock sent her best friend into a spiral of grief and guilt. He replayed every conversation in his mind, tormented by the thought that he should have done more. The questions haunted him: What if I had reached out one more time? What if I had told her she was loved? His grief turned to anger at the bullies who had driven her to despair, and then to rage at himself for staying silent. The weight of guilt crushed him until he turned to substances to numb the pain. What began as an escape soon became a prison of addiction. His life too began to unravel, not because of his own posts, but because of the devastating ripple effect of one life lost to social media cruelty.

Had both Hannah and her friend known the love and salvation of Christ, their stories could have been different. For Christ says:

> *"Come to me, all you who are weary and burdened, and I will give you rest."*
> **Matthew 11:28**

Hannah may have found hope in His promise instead of despair in cruel words. Her friend may have found comfort in the presence of the One who never leaves nor forsakes us, instead of turning to drugs.

Christ is the difference between despair and hope, between death and life, between bondage and freedom.

The Harsh Reality of Social Media

Hannah's story is not an isolated incident, it represents the reality of countless teens today. What happens in silence, in hidden hours of the night, reveals that social media has become a battlefield. According to the Pew Research Center, 46% of U.S. teens say they are online "almost constantly." A 2023 report from the Centers for Disease Control and Prevention revealed that nearly one in three teen girls seriously considered suicide in the past year — the highest level recorded. Suicide is now the second leading cause of death among teens, a staggering statistic that reflects the despair in this generation.

Other studies confirm that peer pressure magnified by social media intensifies feelings of inadequacy. The American Psychological Association warns that social media's culture of likes, comments, and shares often breeds comparison and envy, leading to anxiety and depression. Common Sense Media reports that over 60% of teens say they have been pressured to look or act a certain way because of online standards. The pressure is unrelenting, and many young people live double lives — one carefully curated online for approval, and another offline filled with loneliness and shame. Behind every statistic are names, faces, and families mourning lives stolen by despair magnified through screens.

The Outcasts Christ Redeemed

What social media does today is not new. For generations, society has cast aside those it deemed unworthy, unloved, and unwanted. Yet every time the world labels someone as an outcast, Christ draws near.

Consider the Samaritan woman at the well (John 4). She came in the heat of the day, alone, carrying shame that kept her isolated. Society had written her off as unworthy, but Jesus met her there. He offered her living water and restored her dignity, turning her from an outcast into a witness who brought her whole town to hear the Messiah. Or consider the man possessed by demons in Mark 5, who lived among the tombs, chained and abandoned by his community. Jesus crossed the sea just to reach him, casting out the darkness and clothing him in peace. The world saw a problem, but Christ saw a person worth saving.

Hannah, too, felt cast aside. Her friend, buried in guilt and addiction, felt abandoned. Yet Christ is the same today as He was then. He still meets the broken at the well, the tormented among the tombs, and the lonely behind glowing screens. Where the world says, "You are unworthy," Christ says, "You are mine."

Understanding Human Nature: Body, Soul, and Spirit

Before we can understand the impact of social media and the insidious way it destroys lives, we must first understand who we are as human beings created in the image of God. Scripture reveals that mankind is a three-part being — body, soul, and spirit.

When God formed Adam in the Garden, the Word tells us:

> *"Then the Lord God formed a man from the dust of the ground and breathed into his nostrils the breath of life, and the man became a living being."*
> **Genesis 2:7**

From this moment, we see the mystery of our design. The body was formed from the dust — our physical form, tangible and temporary, returning to the ground in death. The breath of life, God's own Spirit, animated Adam — the spirit is the eternal part of man that communes with God. And the result was that man became a living being — the soul, the seat of the mind, will, and emotions.

The body connects us to the world around us. It experiences hunger, fatigue, pleasure, and pain. It is through the body that we act, speak, and live in the physical realm. Paul reminds us that our bodies are temporary tents (2 Corinthians 5:1), but also temples of the Holy Spirit (1 Corinthians 6:19), meant to glorify God.

The soul is the battleground. It encompasses our thoughts, choices, desires, and feelings. The soul is where temptation is entertained, where decisions are made, and where our true identity is wrestled. It is the essence of who we are — but apart from Christ, it is subject to corruption. Jesus makes clear the soul's eternal value:

> *"What good will it be for someone to gain the whole world, yet forfeit their soul? Or what can anyone give in exchange for their soul?"*
> **Matthew 16:26**

The spirit is the deepest part of man, created to commune with God. It is through the spirit that we experience regeneration when we are born again in Christ (John 3:6). The spirit longs for the presence of God and is made alive by the Holy Spirit. As Hebrews 4:12 declares:

> *"For the word of God is alive and active. Sharper than any double-edged sword, it penetrates even to dividing soul and spirit, joints and marrow; it judges the thoughts and attitudes of the heart."*
> **Hebrews 4:12**

The Word alone is able to cut to the deepest parts of who we are.

When Hannah took her life, her body ceased, but more tragically, her soul was lost without the light of Christ. And this is not only her story — it is a reality for countless teens around us. We as the body of Christ are losing souls daily. Statistics from the Centers for Disease Control and Prevention report that suicide is now the second leading cause of death among teens aged 15–19. In 2021, more than 6,500 young people in this age group took their own lives in the United States alone. Every one of those numbers is not a statistic but a soul — an eternal being, lost to despair before they could encounter the fullness of life in Christ.

This truth should grieve us deeply. It should awaken the Church to the urgency of this moment. We are not fighting against trends, platforms, or algorithms — we are fighting for souls. And each soul matters to God.

Light Versus Darkness

This book is not written to condemn technology itself. Social media is not inherently evil. It is a tool. In the right hands, it can connect families, encourage friendships, and even spread the gospel. But in the wrong hands — or used without wisdom and restraint — it becomes a weapon of destruction, a net that entangles hearts and minds. The true danger lies in how easily it feeds our weaknesses, amplifies temptation, and distracts us from God.

The Scriptures remind us of the seriousness of this battle:

> *"This is the message we have heard from him and declare to you: God is light; in him there is no darkness at all. If we claim to have fellowship with him and yet walk in the darkness, we lie and do not live out the truth. But if we walk in the light, as he is in the light, we have fellowship with one another, and the blood of Jesus, his Son, purifies us from all sin."*
> ***1 John 1:5–7***

Light and darkness are not mere metaphors. In the Bible, light represents truth, holiness, and God's presence, while darkness signifies deception, sin, and separation from Him. Social media promises light — connection, entertainment, recognition — but too often what glitters is only false light, leading to despair. Jesus warns:

> *"When your eyes are healthy, your whole body also is full of light. But when they are unhealthy, your body also is full of darkness. See to it, then, that the light within you is not darkness."*
> ***Luke 11:34–35***

The Battle for the Soul

Here lies the core truth: what appears harmless, even helpful, can quickly enslave when it becomes the source of identity and worth. Social media addiction is not simply a matter of "spending too much time online." It is a spiritual battle that affects the body, the soul, and the spirit.

The body pays the price through sleepless nights, headaches, and stress. The soul — the mind, will, and emotions — becomes restless, disordered, and enslaved to comparison and performance. And the spirit — the deepest part of us, created for communion with God — grows silent, starved for prayer, worship, and truth. Yet Scripture declares that God desires to restore us fully:

> *"May God himself, the God of peace, sanctify you through and through. May your whole spirit, soul and body be kept blameless at the coming of our Lord Jesus Christ."*
> ***1 Thessalonians 5:23***

This is why we cannot dismiss the dangers of digital addiction as trivial. We must name it for what it is: a war for the soul. Jesus asks in Matthew 16:26: "What good will it be for someone to gain the whole world, yet forfeit their soul? Or what can anyone give in exchange for their soul?" To chase after likes, views, and approval while losing the very essence of who we are before God is the greatest tragedy.

The Hope of Christ

Yet this book is not about despair — it is about hope. For in Christ, the battle is already won. He is the true Light who exposes darkness and heals the broken.

> *"When Jesus spoke again to the people, he said, 'I am the light of the world. Whoever follows me will never walk in darkness, but will have the light of life.'"*
> **John 8:12**

Where social media offers only momentary affirmation, Jesus offers eternal belonging. Where screens leave emptiness, He gives rest:

> *"Come to me, all you who are weary and burdened, and I will give you rest. Take my yoke upon you and learn from me, for I am gentle and humble in heart, and you will find rest for your souls."*
> **Matthew 11:28–29**

This book is written for teenagers, their parents, and church leaders. It will explore how the ancient truths of Scripture meet the modern challenges of social media, how the seven deadly sins and the Ten Commandments speak powerfully into our feeds, and how practical steps of assessment, boundaries, and spiritual reset can restore freedom. Each chapter will confront the lies and point to the truth, expose the darkness and call us into the light.

Before you move forward, pause for a moment. Turn off the glow of your device. Take a deep breath. Read this prayer aloud:

> *"The Lord is my light and my salvation — whom shall I fear? The Lord is the stronghold of my life — of whom shall I be afraid?"*
> **Psalm 27:1**

The battle is real. The dangers are insidious. But victory belongs to the Lord, and His light will shine into every dark corner.

CHAPTER 1
THE DARKNESS BEHIND THE SCREEN

God's Truth About Light and Darkness

> *"This is the message we have heard from him and declare to you: God is light; in him there is no darkness at all. If we claim to have fellowship with him and yet walk in the darkness, we lie and do not live out the truth. But if we walk in the light, as he is in the light, we have fellowship with one another, and the blood of Jesus, his Son, purifies us from all sin."*
> ***1 John 1:5–7***

From the very beginning, God separated light from darkness:

> *"God saw that the light was good, and he separated the light from the darkness."*
> **Genesis 1:4**

Light reveals, heals, and gives life, while darkness hides, deceives, and destroys. Social media presents itself as light — a window into the world, a tool for connection. Yet behind the glow of the screen lies darkness: comparison that corrodes joy, envy that poisons gratitude, lust that defiles purity, wrath that wounds with words, and despair that steals life.

The apostle Paul wrote:

> *"For you were once darkness, but now you are light in the Lord. Live as children of light (for the fruit of the light consists in all goodness, righteousness and truth) and find out what pleases the Lord. Have nothing to do with the fruitless deeds of darkness, but rather expose them."*
> **Ephesians 5:8–11**

To walk in the light means to see clearly, to reject the counterfeit, and to expose the darkness for what it is.

Darkness hides behind false light. Jesus warned:

> *"When your eyes are healthy, your whole body also is full of light. But when they are unhealthy, your body also is full of darkness. See to it, then, that the light within you is not darkness."*
> **Luke 11:34–35**

Much of what flashes across screens appears harmless, even good, but often it is false light that blinds and enslaves.

What Is Really Happening Behind the Screens

The glow of social media often appears attractive, but the truth is that many of the influences shaping teens today are profoundly destructive. One of the most insidious is pornography. What was once difficult to obtain is now available in seconds, even for children. Jesus' warning in Matthew 5:28 is clear:

> *"But I tell you that anyone who looks at a woman lustfully has already committed adultery with her in his heart."*
> **Matthew 5:28**

Pornography leads teens into lust, corruption, and addiction.

A 2022 study by Common Sense Media reported that 73% of teens had been exposed to pornography online, many unintentionally, with the average first exposure occurring at just 12 years old. Early exposure rewires how teens view intimacy, often normalizing aggression and teaching distorted views of relationships.

Alongside pornography, cyberbullying thrives on social platforms. Cruel words typed in anonymity wound just as deeply as those spoken aloud. Scripture tells us:

> *"Anyone who hates a brother or sister is a murderer, and you know that no murderer has eternal life residing in him."*
> ***1 John 3:15***

The CDC reports that nearly 16% of high school students in the United States have experienced online bullying, and victims are twice as likely to attempt suicide compared to their peers. The darkness of cyberbullying magnifies despair and has become one of the most lethal weapons against teens today.

Another reality behind the screen is the glorification of substance abuse. Social media is filled with videos glamorizing drinking, vaping, and drug use. Paul reminds us in Ephesians 5:18:

> *"Do not get drunk on wine, which leads to debauchery. Instead, be filled with the Spirit."*
> ***Ephesians 5:18***

Yet teens are persuaded otherwise by influencers and peers who make substance use look fun, harmless, and even necessary for acceptance. The National Institute on Drug Abuse reported in 2023 that nearly 30% of high school seniors admitted to using illicit drugs in the past year, with many saying social media exposure contributed to their curiosity and willingness to try.

Violence and rebellion are also packaged as entertainment online. Teens are drawn into communities where fighting, vandalism, and rebellion against authority are celebrated as bravery. Paul's warning remains timeless:

> *"Do not be misled: 'Bad company corrupts good character.'"*
> **1 Corinthians 15:33**

According to the Office of Juvenile Justice and Delinquency Prevention, teens who consume violent media online are significantly more likely to engage in physical altercations, theft, or gang-related activity. Social media becomes their teacher, and sin becomes their practice.

Finally, there is the confusion surrounding sexuality and gender identity. In a culture where every opinion finds a platform, many teens are discipled more by TikTok influencers than by parents or pastors. God's Word is clear:

> *"Flee from sexual immorality. All other sins a person commits are outside the body, but whoever sins sexually, sins against their own body."*
> **1 Corinthians 6:18**

Yet research from the Trevor Project in 2022 found that over 45% of LGBTQ+ youth seriously considered suicide in the past year, many citing hostile online interactions and identity struggles fueled by comparison and misinformation. Social media, instead of offering clarity, often breeds confusion, isolation, and despair.

Teen Story: The Trap of Pornography

Consider Ethan, a 13-year-old boy who accidentally stumbled upon pornographic content on social media. What shocked him at first soon pulled him back again and again. By the time he was 15, Ethan had grown numb to images that once made him blush. His view of women had been corrupted. He began to objectify every girl he knew, including his own classmates — even his own mother and younger sister no longer commanded his respect.

At 17, driven by lust and fueled by advice from peers and online voices that told him "this is normal," Ethan forced himself on a girl he was dating. He was arrested and convicted of date rape. His life, the life of his victim, and the peace of his family were shattered. What began with a single click at 13 became a prison of shame and destruction at 17.

Sadly, Ethan's story reflects reality. Research shows that more than 70% of boys and 60% of girls are exposed to pornography before age 18. Many are first exposed through social media feeds. Studies also show that early exposure to pornography is linked to aggressive sexual behavior, risky encounters, and distorted relationships.

A Biblical Parallel: Amnon and Tamar

The tragedy of Ethan mirrors a story from Scripture. In 2 Samuel 13, Amnon, one of King David's sons, became obsessed with his half-sister Tamar. Instead of resisting sin, he listened to bad advice from his cousin Jonadab, who told him how to lure her into his chamber. Blinded by lust, Amnon raped Tamar. The act devastated her life and brought ruin upon David's household.

Just as Amnon followed Jonadab's corrupt advice, teens today follow the corrupt voices they encounter online. Social media platforms serve as modern-day

Jonadabs, whispering lies, encouraging sin, and justifying rebellion against God. The result is the same: broken lives, shattered families, and souls lost in darkness.

The Reality of Devastation

The impact is undeniable. A 2023 CDC report revealed that suicide is now the second leading cause of death among teens, and teen girls in particular report record levels of hopelessness. Studies show that teens who spend more than seven hours daily online are twice as likely to be diagnosed with depression or anxiety compared to those who limit screen time. Pornography addiction, bullying, and toxic advice magnify despair and lead many into destructive paths.

But the good news is this: the darkness is not the end of the story. Jesus declares:

> *"I am the light of the world. Whoever follows me will never walk in darkness, but will have the light of life."*
> ***John 8:12***

He does not simply reveal sin; He redeems sinners. He does not merely expose bondage; He sets captives free. The light of Christ is greater than the glow of any screen.

The Word as Our Guide

> *"Your word is a lamp for my feet, a light on my path."*
> **Psalm 119:105**

God's Word, not the endless scroll, shows the way forward. A teenager who begins the day not with notifications but with Scripture takes the first step toward freedom. A family who chooses to set aside devices at mealtimes experiences fellowship as God intended it. A church that teaches teens not just to resist temptation but to delight in the light of Christ arms a generation for victory.

The body, soul, and spirit all find healing in His light. The body receives rest when we obey His rhythms of Sabbath. The soul finds order when the truth renews the mind. The spirit comes alive when worship reclaims its rightful place. Paul prayed:

> *"May God himself, the God of peace, sanctify you through and through. May your whole spirit, soul and body be kept blameless at the coming of our Lord Jesus Christ."*
> **1 Thessalonians 5:23**

That is God's desire — not fragmented lives, but wholeness in Him.

Chapter 1 Reflection

Imagine ending your day with this prayer from Psalm 4:

> *"In peace I will lie down and sleep, for you alone, Lord, make me dwell in safety."*
> **Psalm 4:8**

Place the phone away, close your eyes, and let His Word be the last voice you hear. That is not small; it is the beginning of life walking in the light.

CHAPTER 2
THE SEVEN DEADLY SINS IN THE DIGITAL AGE

The Wages of Sin Is Death

From the earliest days of the Church, believers named seven deadly sins: pride, envy, wrath, sloth, greed, lust, and gluttony. They were called deadly not because they kill instantly but because they eat away at the soul, drawing it further from God. Paul makes this truth plain in Romans 6:23:

> *"For the wages of sin is death, but the gift of God is eternal life in Christ Jesus our Lord."*
> **Romans 6:23**

Sin is not harmless entertainment or a minor mistake — it carries within it the seed of death.

This reality is not new. From the beginning of creation, God warned Adam and Eve in the garden:

> *"You must not eat from the tree of the knowledge of good and evil, for when you eat from it you will certainly die."*
> **Genesis 2:17**

Yet when tempted, they disobeyed, and the curse of sin and death entered the world. Their bodies began to decay, their souls were corrupted by shame and fear, and their spirits were separated from God. That same curse is at work today, and social media has become one of the most insidious instruments by which sin multiplies among the young.

In the digital age, the seven deadly sins are not distant concepts but daily temptations. Teens scrolling through their phones encounter pride in self-promotion, envy in comparison, wrath in comment wars, sloth in endless scrolling, greed in consumerism, lust in explicit content, and gluttony in digital overindulgence. Each sin promises pleasure but delivers bondage. Each sin wounds the body, disorders the soul, and starves the spirit.

Pride: The Performance of Self

Pride is the sin of exalting oneself above others, seeking recognition and honor rather than humility before God. Proverbs warns:

> *"When pride comes, then comes disgrace, but with humility comes wisdom."*
> **Proverbs 11:2**

Social media magnifies this sin by making every moment an opportunity for self-promotion. Likes, shares, and followers become a false currency of value.

For teens, this performance of self creates crushing pressure. According to the Pew Research Center, nearly 40% of teens admit they feel anxious about whether people will like their posts. One high school girl, Kayla, confessed that she deleted dozens of pictures that did not receive enough likes. She equated low engagement with being unworthy. This constant need for approval eroded her confidence and filled her with shame.

In the Bible, pride led to Nebuchadnezzar's downfall. After boasting in his glory and the power of Babylon, he was struck down by God, driven away from people, and forced to live like an animal until he acknowledged God's sovereignty (Daniel 4:30–32). Like Kayla, Nebuchadnezzar's pride made him believe his value rested in his own image, not in God. Both stories remind us that pride enslaves the soul, wears down the body with anxiety, and starves the spirit of humility before the Lord.

Envy: The Poison of Comparison

Envy is the sin of desiring what others have and resenting their blessings. James warns:

> *"For where you have envy and selfish ambition, there you find disorder and every evil practice."*
> **James 3:16**

Social media is fertile soil for envy, with endless highlight reels of vacations, beauty, and success.

Teens scrolling through these illusions measure themselves and come up empty.

The American Psychological Association has found that heavy social media use is strongly linked to depression because of comparison. Daniel, a fifteen-year-old boy, spent hours scrolling through posts of classmates wearing expensive sneakers and driving new cars. Convinced he was inferior, he grew bitter toward his parents for not providing more. His soul was robbed of gratitude, and his joy evaporated.

Scripture warns us through the story of Cain and Abel. Cain envied his brother because God accepted Abel's offering but not his. Instead of repenting, Cain let envy fester until it led to murder (Genesis 4:5–8). Like Cain, Daniel's envy consumed him, corroding his soul and creating bitterness in his heart. Envy may begin in the eyes, but it quickly poisons the soul and separates us from God's peace.

Wrath: The Violence of Words

Wrath is uncontrolled anger expressed in ways that wound and destroy. James counsels:

> *"Everyone should be quick to listen, slow to speak and slow to become angry, because human anger does not produce the righteousness that God desires."*
> **James 1:19–20**

On social media, wrath erupts daily through insults, cancel culture, and bullying.

The CDC reports that nearly 16% of high school students have been victims of cyberbullying. Chloe, a bright and outgoing teen, was repeatedly targeted with cruel messages about her appearance. Her self-esteem collapsed, and she began to lash out at her family in anger. The wrath poured onto her online turned inward, filling her soul with bitterness and her body with stress.

In the Bible, King Saul's wrath toward David destroyed his reign. Consumed with jealousy, Saul hurled spears at David and pursued him relentlessly (1 Samuel 18:8–9). Just as Saul's wrath blinded him to God's blessing, Chloe's bullies were blinded by their anger and cruelty. Wrath poisons both the one who inflicts it and the one who receives it, corroding body, soul, and spirit alike.

Sloth: The Idleness of Endless Scrolling

Sloth is more than laziness; it is spiritual neglect, the refusal to act on what God has called us to do. Proverbs rebukes the sluggard:

> *"A little sleep, a little slumber, a little folding of the hands to rest — and poverty will come on you like a thief."*
> ***Proverbs 6:10–11***

Teens today lose entire nights to scrolling, wasting the hours meant for rest, service, and growth.

A seventeen-year-old named Marcus admitted that he often stayed awake until three in the morning watching videos, only to sleep through class and fail assignments. He missed soccer practice, lost his spot on the team, and became apathetic about life. His body weakened, his soul lost direction, and his spirit no longer hungered for God.

Scripture tells of the servant in the parable of the talents who buried his master's gift out of idleness. When the master returned, he condemned the servant's sloth, casting him out (Matthew 25:26–30). Like that servant, Marcus squandered his opportunities. Sloth numbs the soul, dulls the spirit, and wastes the body until life itself becomes barren.

Greed: The Hunger for More

Greed is the craving for possessions and wealth beyond what God provides. Jesus warns:

> *"Watch out! Be on your guard against all kinds of greed; life does not consist in an abundance of possessions."*
> **Luke 12:15**

Social media glorifies greed with ads and influencers presenting material wealth as the key to happiness.

Sophia, a sixteen-year-old girl, became obsessed with owning luxury clothes after watching influencers online. She begged her parents to buy what they could not afford and grew resentful when they refused. She secretly stole money from her mother's purse, convinced it would buy her acceptance. Instead, it fractured her family's trust and burdened her soul with guilt.

The Bible shows greed most starkly in Judas Iscariot. For thirty pieces of silver, he betrayed the Lord (Matthew 26:14–15). Like Judas, Sophia exchanged relationship for possessions. Greed enslaves, breaking down the body through constant striving, consuming the soul with discontent, and leaving the spirit barren of gratitude.

Lust: The Corruption of Desire

Lust is disordered desire that reduces others to objects of gratification. Jesus said:

> *"Anyone who looks at a woman lustfully has already committed adultery with her in his heart."*
> **Matthew 5:28**

Social media is saturated with sexual images that inflame lust, shaping teens' views of intimacy and relationships.

Jacob, a fourteen-year-old boy, confessed that after months of watching explicit videos online, he could no longer see girls at school as people but only as objects. His grades slipped, friendships dissolved, and his family relationships suffered. His body became addicted, his soul was weighed down with shame, and his spirit drifted far from God.

In Scripture, lust led David to take Bathsheba for himself, leading to adultery, deception, and the murder of her husband (2 Samuel 11). Just as David's lust brought destruction to his kingdom, Jacob's lust devastated his young life. Lust promises excitement but delivers ruin to body, soul, and spirit.

Gluttony: The Overconsumption of Content

Gluttony is excess, the inability to say "enough." Paul exhorts:

> *"So whether you eat or drink or whatever you do, do it all for the glory of God."*
> **1 Corinthians 10:31**

In the digital world, gluttony appears in binge-watching, endless gaming, and consuming content without rest or moderation.

Emma, a teenager, admitted to spending an entire weekend consuming videos and shows. By Monday, she was exhausted, behind in homework, and filled with emptiness. Her body was fatigued, her soul was dull, and her spirit was untouched by prayer or worship.

The Israelites in the wilderness fell into gluttony when they grumbled for more meat though God had given them manna (Numbers 11:4–6). Their overindulgence provoked God's judgment. Like Israel, Emma consumed far more than she needed, and the result was not fulfillment but emptiness. Digital gluttony promises satisfaction but leaves only spiritual starvation.

Christ, the Freedom from Sin

Each of these sins wages war on the body, soul, and spirit. Pride enslaves the soul to self. Envy robs the emotions of joy. Wrath poisons relationships and burdens the body with stress. Sloth weakens the will and dulls the spirit. Greed cultivates discontent that eats away at the heart. Lust desecrates the body and deadens the spirit. Gluttony numbs the soul and leaves no room for God.

But Christ offers freedom. Where pride rules, humility in Christ brings wisdom. Where envy eats away, adoption in Christ restores security. Where wrath rages, gentleness bears fruit. Where sloth paralyzes, love empowers service. Where greed enslaves, generosity frees. Where lust ensnares, purity redeems. Where gluttony overwhelms, self-control restores balance.

Chapter 2 Reflection

This week, take one of these sins that most entangles you and confess it to God. Replace it with its opposite virtue. Read this aloud:

> *"So if the Son sets you free, you will be free indeed."*
> **John 8:36**

Trust that in Him, no chain is unbreakable.

CHAPTER 3
THE TEN COMMANDMENTS AND THE BATTLE FOR THE SOUL

The Ten Commandments are not relics of the past. They are the living Word of God, revealing His holiness, guarding His people from harm, and pointing us to life. Each speaks powerfully to the struggles teens face in the digital age.

> *"You shall have no other gods before me."*
> **Exodus 20:3**

When social media becomes the source of identity and purpose, it is an idol. God alone deserves our worship.

> *"You shall not make for yourself an image."*
> **Exodus 20:4**

Carefully curated online personas can become false images that enslave us. But we are already made in God's image (Genesis 1:27).

> *"You shall not misuse the name of the Lord your God."*
> **Exodus 20:7**

God's name is mocked daily online. His name is holy and must be honored.

> *"Remember the Sabbath day by keeping it holy."*
> **Exodus 20:8**

Endless scrolling robs us of rest. God commands Sabbath for our good, that our bodies, souls, and spirits may be renewed.

> *"Honor your father and your mother."*
> **Exodus 20:12**

Online rebellion often manifests as dishonor. But God attaches a promise:

> *"so that you may live long in the land the Lord your God is giving you." "You shall not murder."*
> **Exodus 20:13**

Words kill as surely as weapons. Cyberbullying has driven many to despair and even suicide. Jesus deepened this command:

> *"Anyone who is angry with a brother or sister will be subject to judgment."*
> **Matthew 5:22**

> *"You shall not commit adultery."*
> **Exodus 20:14**

Lust, pornography, and sexual sin are rampant online. Jesus declared:

> *"Anyone who looks at a woman lustfully has already committed adultery with her in his heart."*
> **Matthew 5:28**

> *"You shall not steal."*
> **Exodus 20:15**

Digital culture normalizes piracy, plagiarism, and theft of content. But God calls His people to integrity.

> *"You shall not give false testimony."*
> **Exodus 20:16**

Lies, gossip, and fake news are common online. Yet God calls us to speak truth in love (Ephesians 4:15).

> *"You shall not covet."*
> **Exodus 20:17**

Social media trains hearts to desire what others have. But Scripture reminds us,

> *"Keep your lives free from the love of money and be content with what you have, because God has said, 'Never will I leave you; never will I forsake you.'"*
> **Hebrews 13:5**

The commandments expose sin, but they also point us to Christ. Paul wrote,

> *"Therefore no one will be declared righteous in God's sight by the works of the law; rather, through the law we become conscious of our sin."*
> **Romans 3:20**

The law reveals our need, and Christ fulfills it.

The soul is the battleground. The body craves comfort and pleasure, the spirit longs for holiness, and the soul—the seat of mind, will, and emotions—is caught in between. Jesus asked,

> *"What good will it be for someone to gain the whole world, yet forfeit their soul?"*
> **Matthew 16:26**

Social media offers the illusion of gaining the world, but the danger is losing the soul.

Sinai and the Gift of the Law

Israel did not receive commandments in a vacuum. God rescued them from slavery with a mighty hand, split the sea, and brought them to Himself at Sinai. Thunder rolled, fire fell, and a trembling people stood at the base of the mountain while Moses ascended to hear the voice of the Lord. The tablets were written by the very finger of God, not to crush freedom but to preserve it. The first four commands teach us to love and honor the Lord; the last six teach us to love and honor people. The law reveals that life flourishes only under God's rule and in God's ways.

Love Fulfills the Law

When Jesus was asked which commandment was greatest, He replied,

> *"Love the Lord your God with all your heart and with all your soul and with all your mind...And the second is like it: Love your neighbor as yourself. All the Law and the Prophets hang on these two commandments."*
> ***Matthew 22:37–40***

If we love God first, we will not put another god before Him, fashion an image to replace Him, profane His name, or trample His Sabbath.

If we love our neighbor, we will honor parents, protect life and purity, respect property and truth, and guard the heart against coveting. Love is not sentiment; it is obedience shaped by the cross. Social media often runs on something other than love—it runs on envy and outrage, on pride and performance. Scripture counters the digital storm with a simple, blazing sentence:

> *"Above all, love each other deeply, because love covers over a multitude of sins."*
> ***1 Peter 4:8***

"You Shall Have No Other Gods Before Me"
Idolatry in the Age of the Feed

Idolatry in a teen's life can look like the phone that is checked before prayer, the feed that sets worth before God does, the audience that determines identity before the Father speaks. Surveys show that U.S. teens now average nearly five hours daily on social platforms, with half spending four hours or more every day. Such immersion forms loves and loyalties, often without notice, and the heart becomes bound to the approval of strangers. (Gallup.com)

Alex learned this the hard way. His morning liturgy was not Scripture but checking notifications. When his account was hacked and erased, he felt as though his life had been erased with it. The idol crashed and left him hollow. Israel knew this path when they forged a golden calf to worship in the very shadow of Sinai. The counterfeit always promises control and gives chains instead. Idolatry aligns with the deadly sins of pride and envy, feeding on performance and comparison. It burdens the body with anxiety, disorients the soul with fear, and estranges the spirit from communion with God.

"You Shall Not Make for Yourself an Image"
Curated Selves and Splintered Souls

False images do not require gold; they require filters. Teens are tempted to live split lives—one face for home, another for the hidden account. The pressure to maintain a persona extracts a toll that shows up as sleepless nights, sadness, and shame. National surveys continue to document widespread teen distress; in the wake of the pandemic, more than two in five high-school students reported persistent feelings of sadness or hopelessness, with teen girls bearing a disproportionate burden. (CDC)

Samantha perfected two personas, polished and reckless, and keeping both afloat fractured her peace. Jeroboam once set up images that were easier to follow than the living God, and generations stumbled after him. A digital mask can feel safer than the face God gave, yet it splinters the soul. Pride and deceit are its companions; the body shows the strain in fatigue, the soul in anxiety, and the spirit in distance from truth.

"You Shall Not Misuse the Name of the Lord"
Reverence in a Culture of Casual

When God's name becomes a meme, reverence erodes. Teens absorb thousands of casual invocations that make the Holy ordinary. Jacob laughed at irreverent jokes until the laughter numbed his sense of sacred. Scripture treated blasphemy with gravity because names bear presence.

To normalize irreverence is to train the tongue and the heart to forget who God is. Though there is no national metric for profanity, the broader patterns of teen mental and spiritual distress remind us that what saturates the eyes and ears shapes the heart. The deadly sins here are pride and gluttony of content—saying anything, consuming everything—and the cost is a dulled spirit.

"Remember the Sabbath Day"
Rest in a World That Never Stops

Sabbath is God's remedy for restless bodies, harried souls, and hungry spirits. But phones glow long past midnight, and sleep slips away. Recent CDC reports indicate that roughly seven in ten high-school students get insufficient sleep on school nights, a pattern tied to worse mental and physical health. (CDC)

Ethan never stopped scrolling. By Sunday his mind drifted in worship and his body sagged in class. Israel's neglect of Sabbath drew rebuke because rest is not optional for creatures; it is commanded for their good. Sloth and gluttony intertwine here—not mere laziness, but compulsive overconsumption—and the result is depletion of body, disorder of soul, and dryness of spirit.

"Honor Your Father and Your Mother"
Reverence at Home in a World of Rebroadcast

Honor is the habit of ascribing weight to parents. Social media urges teens to broadcast private conflicts for laughs or likes. Lily built a following by mocking her parents' rules on video; the crowd's cheer drowned out the fifth commandment's promise. Absalom's rebellion against David shows how dishonor tears families and nations.

Pride and wrath often fuel this sin online, turning the heart away from the first community God designed. The body feels the stress of constant conflict, the soul hardens in contempt, and the spirit resists authority, even the Lord's.

"You Shall Not Murder"
The Weight of Words and the Wounds They Leave

Jesus locates murder in the heart long before a hand is raised. On the internet, anger travels at light speed, and taunting can crush the breath from a teen's hope. National data show that a sizeable share of students report bullying, and recent YRBS trends highlight concerning increases in violence indicators alongside pervasive mental-health strain; teen girls in particular report very high levels of sadness and serious consideration of suicide. (CDC)

Sophie endured a barrage of posts that mocked her body and faith. The classmates who typed the words never touched her, but what they wrote injured her life. Cain's envy of Abel flowered into violence; today, wrath rides the algorithm. The deadly sin is wrath, but envy and pride are close by. The body registers chronic stress, the soul absorbs shame, and the spirit grows numb. The sixth commandment calls us back to love's protection of life.

"You Shall Not Commit Adultery"
Purity in a Hypersexualized Stream

Jesus calls lust adultery of the heart. Social media exposes teens to sexual content that reshapes desire and sears conscience. National child-protection data show the scale of online exploitation: in 2023 alone, the CyberTipline received more than 36 million reports, with online enticement cases surging dramatically in recent years and over 100 million suspected abuse files flagged. While these reports span many ages, they underscore the digital environment teens inhabit and the ease with which predators and explicit content reach youth. (NCMEC, Thorn)

Michael started by following suggestive accounts and ended by pressuring his girlfriend to cross lines she later wept over. David's gaze toward Bathsheba became a chain of sins with devastating fallout. The deadly sin here is lust; greed and gluttony of content often accompany it. The body becomes enslaved to dopamine cycles, the soul is shackled by guilt and distorted affections, and the spirit withdraws from the presence in which purity is restored.

"You Shall Not Steal"
Integrity When Everything Feels "Free"

Digital theft wears many faces: pirating shows and software, lifting creators' work, and submitting unearned words as one's own. Schools report that academic dishonesty in the era of AI has become a live and rising concern, with a recent national teacher survey noting a sharp increase in students getting in trouble for suspected AI-aided work during the 2023–24 year. The point is not technology but integrity; theft corrodes trust and character, even when the victim is invisible. (Education Week)

Noah copied essays he found online and turned them in as his own until a teacher confronted him and consequences followed. Achan's hidden theft in Jericho brought defeat to a whole community. The deadly sins of greed and sloth mingle here: wanting reward without labor. The body may feel the fleeting relief of cutting corners, but the soul weakens in dishonesty and the spirit grieves.

"You Shall Not Give False Testimony"
Truth in an Age of Virality

False testimony today looks like a rumor shared as fact, a doctored image passed along, an accusation that outruns evidence. Emily's post about a classmate started as a joke and metastasized into a scandal that damaged reputations for months. False witness helped condemn Jesus; lies still crucify truth. OJJDP's national literature review on bullying and cyberbullying summarizes a field in which electronic harassment, rumor-spreading, and social exclusion are common components of harm, particularly for girls, and persist as a measurable problem across years. (purl.fdlp.gov)

The deadly sins of pride and envy fuel false witness; wrath often spreads it. The body learns to live in adrenaline, the soul becomes comfortable with distortion, and the spirit loses appetite for the God whose very name is Truth.

"You Shall Not Covet"
Desire Retrained by Gratitude

Coveting is desire turned against love. Feeds full of highlight reels teach teens to want another's body, home, vacations, or platform. National polling shows that teens spend hours a day in these curated environments; the more time immersed, the more comparison becomes the default lens. (Gallup.com)

Ben followed an influencer whose life seemed effortless and glamorous. After months of daily viewing, his own life felt small and bitter. Ahab coveted Naboth's vineyard until coveting became conspiracy and blood. The deadly sin here is envy, and its fruit is restlessness. The body aches under stress, the soul forgets contentment, and the spirit cannot lift its eyes in worship. The tenth commandment invites a new habit of heart: to behold God's gifts and be satisfied.

Chapter 3 Reflection

The commandments expose sin, but they also point us to Christ.

> *"Therefore no one will be declared righteous in God's sight by the works of the law; rather, through the law we become conscious of our sin."*
> **Romans 3:20**

The law brings us to the cross, where the curse is lifted and a new obedience is born. The soul is the battleground. The body craves comfort and pleasure, the spirit longs for holiness, and the soul—the seat of mind, will, and emotions—is caught in between. Jesus asks every generation,

> *"What good will it be for someone to gain the whole world, yet forfeit their soul?"*
> **Matthew 16:26**

Social media offers the illusion of gaining the world, but the danger is losing the soul. This is why the Church must call teens higher and nearer.

Read each of the Ten Commandments aloud this week. After each, pray quietly, "Lord, write this on my heart." Let love drive your obedience, because love fulfills the law, and love covers a multitude of sins. And if anyone looks down on you because of your age, remember Paul's charge:

> *"Don't let anyone look down on you because you are young, but set an example for the believers in speech, in conduct, in love, in faith and in purity."*
> **1 Timothy 4:12**

CHAPTER 4
ADDICTION, DEVIANCE, AND SPIRITUAL WARFARE

Addiction as Enslavement

> *"Jesus replied, 'Very truly I tell you, everyone who sins is a slave to sin. Now a slave has no permanent place in the family, but a son belongs to it forever. So if the Son sets you free, you will be free indeed.'"*
> ***John 8:34–36***

Addiction is enslavement. It is the condition in which something once chosen becomes something that controls you. Medical science describes addiction as the rewiring of the brain's reward system. At the center of this system is dopamine, the chemical messenger of pleasure and reward. When dopamine is released, the brain feels satisfied and reinforced to repeat the behavior that triggered it. This is normal when eating a meal, achieving a goal, or sharing in healthy community. But when the system is hijacked, what was meant for good becomes destructive.

Social media hijacks this system. Each notification, like, heart, or comment releases a surge of dopamine, creating a small "high." Because likes and shares are unpredictable, the brain becomes even more addicted — waiting, refreshing, anticipating. This intermittent reinforcement, neuroscientists say, is the same principle behind slot machines. It keeps users hooked, endlessly checking for the next rush of affirmation.

For teens, whose brains are still developing, this cycle is especially dangerous. The prefrontal cortex — the region of the brain responsible for impulse control and long-term decision-making — is not fully mature until around age 25. This means adolescents are more vulnerable to the pull of dopamine-driven behaviors. A "like" on a post is not just harmless approval; it is a biochemical reward that teaches the teen's brain to keep coming back for more.

Consider the spiritual dimension: what science calls dopamine-driven behavior, Scripture calls slavery. Paul wrote:

> *"Do you not know that when you offer yourselves to someone as obedient slaves, you are slaves of the one you obey—whether you are slaves to sin, which leads to death, or to obedience, which leads to righteousness?"*
> **Romans 6:16**

Teens who live for likes and attention are not only chemically bound but spiritually trapped. Approval has become an idol, and dopamine has become its sacrament.

Deviant Behavior Defined

Deviant behavior is not a neutral term. In sociology, deviance refers to actions that break social norms and expectations. But Scripture goes deeper, identifying deviance as rebellion against God's commands. Disobedience, dishonor, impurity, violence, and deceit are not simply maladjustments to culture; they are evidence of sin and spiritual bondage.

Paul described the root:

> *"The acts of the flesh are obvious: sexual immorality, impurity and debauchery; idolatry and witchcraft; hatred, discord, jealousy, fits of rage, selfish ambition, dissensions, factions and envy; drunkenness, orgies, and the like. I warn you, as I did before, that those who live like this will not inherit the kingdom of God."*
> **Galatians 5:19–21**

Deviance is sin manifested in life, and social media has become a stage upon which these sins are celebrated and normalized.

Researchers have documented the link between social media use, addiction, and deviance. According to the CDC, teens who spend more than five to seven hours a day online are twice as likely to experience depression, engage in risky behaviors, and report violent altercations. The Department of Justice warns that online platforms often become environments where cyberbullying, sexting, and peer-driven delinquency flourish. Addiction lays the foundation; deviance is its fruit.

Deviance as Spiritual Warfare

Paul reminds us:

> *"For our struggle is not against flesh and blood, but against the rulers, against the authorities, against the powers of this dark world and against the spiritual forces of evil in the heavenly realms."*
> ***Ephesians 6:12)***

Behind every act of disobedience is a spiritual war for the soul.

When a teen spends hours immersed in content that glorifies rebellion, that is not merely cultural influence — it is spiritual indoctrination. When envy steals joy from scrolling through highlight reels, that is not simply low self-esteem — it is a demonic foothold. When lust is inflamed by pornography, that is not merely curiosity — it is a spirit of bondage.

And dopamine is the hook. What begins as the thrill of being noticed becomes a habit, then a craving, then a stronghold. Teens are tempted to check their phones constantly, not just to connect with friends but to feed the craving of their bodies and emotions. The devil uses what feels like harmless scrolling to train hearts toward idolatry and away from intimacy with God.

Jordan, a sixteen-year-old, admitted that the thrill of each new like on his TikTok videos became addictive. At first, he enjoyed making funny clips. But soon he felt worthless if a video did not "go viral." He grew angry at his parents for asking him to take breaks, rebellious against his teachers, and distant from church. His story illustrates how dopamine craving can open the door to rebellion, deviance, and spiritual strongholds.

The Israelites in the wilderness repeatedly turned to rebellion after deliverance from Egypt. Despite God's miracles, they craved the food and comfort of slavery more than the freedom of obedience (Numbers 11). Their cravings led to disobedience and judgment. In the same way, the craving for digital affirmation enslaves many teens, leading them into patterns of rebellion and sin.

The Cost of Body, Soul, and Spirit

Addiction and deviance exact a heavy toll. The body becomes restless and ill. The CDC reports that over 70% of teens fail to get adequate sleep on school nights, with screen use a primary cause. Sleeplessness contributes to headaches, obesity, and chronic stress.

The soul becomes fractured. The American Psychological Association has found strong links between social media addiction and anxiety, depression, and loneliness. Teens describe feeling "empty" without their phones, enslaved to impulses, and consumed by comparison.

The spirit suffers most. As prayer is replaced with posts and worship with scrolling, teens are starved of communion with God. The thrill of dopamine is temporary; the hunger of the spirit remains unsatisfied. Paul's warning is sobering:

> *"Do not give the devil a foothold."*
> **Ephesians 4:27**

Each unchecked craving, each compromise, and each indulgence in digital affirmation opens the door wider to spiritual deception.

Victory in the Armor of God

Though the battle is fierce, God has not left His people defenseless. Paul wrote:

> *"Finally, be strong in the Lord and in his mighty power. Put on the full armor of God, so that you can take your stand against the devil's schemes."*
> **Ephesians 6:10–11**

The belt of truth counters lies; the breastplate of righteousness guards against shame; the gospel of peace steadies against fear; the shield of faith extinguishes doubt; the helmet of salvation protects the mind; and the sword of the Spirit cuts through deception.

Sarah was consumed by online bullying. The insults triggered dopamine cravings — she would check obsessively to see what was being said, even though it hurt her. Soon she lashed out at her parents and withdrew from faith. But when she discovered the armor of God in Ephesians 6, she began to fight differently. By memorizing Scripture and resisting the urge to seek validation online, she found peace where there had been torment.

Jesus Himself faced the enemy's lies in the wilderness (Matthew 4:1–11). Satan tempted Him with shortcuts to approval, glory, and power. But Jesus answered with Scripture. Where teens today often fall for the promise of instant affirmation, Christ shows that truth and obedience defeat lies.

Chapter 4 Reflection

Pause here and reflect: where has deviant behavior crept into your life? Have you allowed anger, lust, envy, or rebellion to become habits? Confess them honestly to God. Then pray through Ephesians 6:10–18, asking Him to clothe you with the full armor of God.

Deviant behavior is not simply a matter of bad choices. It is the evidence of a battle being lost in the soul. But through Christ, victory is possible.

> *"The light shines in the darkness, and the darkness has not overcome it."*
> **John 1:5**

CHAPTER 5
BOUNDARIES AND SPIRITUAL RESET

Addiction is broken not by willpower alone but by boundaries set in wisdom and by spiritual renewal through Christ. Social media's pull is strong, but Scripture offers guidance for how to resist and reset.

The Need for Boundaries

Paul wrote,

> *"'I have the right to do anything,' you say — but not everything is beneficial. 'I have the right to do anything' — but I will not be mastered by anything."*
> ***1 Corinthians 6:12***

Freedom in Christ is not permission for slavery. Boundaries are not chains; they are guards against bondage. A boundary is a holy line drawn around the heart and life, not to keep freedom out but to keep captivity away.

In today's digital age, boundaries are desperately needed. Social media companies design their platforms to keep teens scrolling. The average U.S. teenager now spends more than four and a half hours per day on social platforms, with many spending over seven hours. Studies show that teens who use social media excessively are far more likely to suffer from depression, anxiety, and sleep deprivation. The CDC reports that more than 70 percent of high school students fail to get enough sleep, with late-night screen use a primary cause.

For teens, boundaries might look like turning off devices an hour before bedtime, limiting daily screen time to two hours, or even choosing one day each week as a Sabbath from technology. Some need to set boundaries on the number of "friends" they keep online. Pew Research has shown that the average teen reports hundreds of connections on social media, but the vast majority of those relationships are superficial. In reality, most teens have never even met the people they call "friends." Proverbs warns,

> *"One who has unreliable friends soon comes to ruin, but there is a friend who sticks closer than a brother."*
> **Proverbs 18:24**

Social media offers quantity without quality, connection without commitment.

Boundaries protect not only time but also relationships. They safeguard the heart from chasing approval and from being mastered by endless digital chatter. Jesus Himself modeled boundaries. Luke 5:16 tells us, "But Jesus often withdrew to lonely places and prayed." Even the Son of God set aside crowds and voices to be alone with the Father. Teens today must learn that stepping away from their feeds is not weakness but wisdom, not withdrawal but worship.

Emily, a high school junior, realized her social media use was stealing her sleep and her joy. She decided, with her parents' help, to set a boundary: no phone after 9:00 p.m. At first she felt anxious, afraid she would miss out. But after a few weeks she noticed her grades improving, her moods stabilizing, and her time with God growing richer. The boundary became a blessing.

Daniel, taken captive to Babylon, faced pressure to consume what everyone else was consuming at the king's table. Yet he resolved not to defile himself (Daniel 1:8). Daniel's boundary preserved his integrity and opened the door to God's favor. In the same way, teens who dare to resist the consumption that culture demands are often the ones whom God uses most powerfully.

The Call to Spiritual Reset

Boundaries alone, however, are not enough. Addiction cannot be broken by restriction only; it requires renewal. Paul urged believers:

> *"Do not conform to the pattern of this world, but be transformed by the renewing of your mind."*
> **Romans 12:2**

A spiritual reset is more than willpower; it is a return of the soul to God.

Reset begins with repentance. It requires acknowledging that addiction to screens and approval has taken God's rightful place in the heart. Repentance clears the soil for new growth. Reset continues with renewal. Just as fasting from food turns hunger into prayer, fasting from social media can redirect cravings toward God. Jesus declared,

> *"Man shall not live on bread alone, but on every word that comes from the mouth of God."*
> **Matthew 4:4**

Teens who set aside even a week from social media often find themselves restless at first, but that hunger can become an invitation to feast on the Word instead.

Reset is sustained by communion. Worship, prayer, Scripture, and fellowship with God's people must fill the spaces once consumed by screens. David prayed,

> *"Create in me a pure heart, O God, and renew a steadfast spirit within me."*
> **Psalm 51:10**

A reset restores purity, renews steadfastness, and reorders life under God's reign.

Marcus was addicted to likes. Every post he made was a bid for attention. But when his youth group began a 21-day "reset challenge" — fasting from social media and replacing it with Scripture reading and journaling — Marcus experienced withdrawal at first. He confessed that he reached for his phone over and over again, only to remember the challenge. Yet by the end of three weeks, he testified that he felt more peace than he had in years, and he was hearing God's voice in ways he had forgotten were possible.

After Israel repeatedly rebelled, God called them to reset:

> *"If my people, who are called by my name, will humble themselves and pray and seek my face and turn from their wicked ways, then I will hear from heaven, and I will forgive their sin and will heal their land."*
> ***2 Chronicles 7:14***

Reset is not merely individual but communal. Families, youth groups, and churches can reset together, choosing to fast from digital noise and feast on the presence of God.

Body, Soul, and Spirit Restored

When boundaries are set and resets embraced, restoration flows into every part of life. The body begins to heal as sleep returns and stress decreases. The CDC notes that adequate sleep improves academic performance, athletic ability, and emotional stability. The soul finds peace when comparison and noise are silenced; the mind is renewed, the emotions steadied, and the will strengthened. The spirit awakens when prayer, worship, and Scripture reclaim attention once wasted on the scroll.

Toward Genuine Relationships

One of the greatest dangers of social media is the illusion of friendship. Teens may have hundreds or even thousands of connections, yet feel profoundly lonely. Research confirms this paradox: despite unprecedented connectivity, Generation Z reports the highest levels of loneliness in recorded history. Proverbs 18:24 warns that too many unreliable friends lead to ruin, but true friendship — the kind that sticks closer than a brother — is rare. Social media multiplies the unreliable and obscures the real.

Boundaries help clear the way for genuine relationships. When teens limit online connections and invest in face-to-face community, they discover depth where once there was only breadth. When a teen chooses to spend less time scrolling and more time in person with family or church friends, the soul is nourished in ways that digital approval can never match.

Sophie had over a thousand online friends, but when she went through a family crisis, only two people showed up for her in person. She realized that what she had was not true friendship but a digital mirage. By setting boundaries and investing in youth group relationships, Sophie discovered friends who prayed with her, laughed with her, and stood by her.

Jesus Himself modeled genuine friendship with His disciples. Though multitudes followed Him, He chose twelve to walk closely with Him and three — Peter, James, and John — to share His most intimate moments. True friendship is not measured in numbers but in depth, sacrifice, and presence.

Chapter 5 Reflection

Where in your life do you need boundaries? What would a spiritual reset look like for you? Begin with one step: choose a time, a place, and a practice that will draw your body, soul, and spirit back to God. Pray David's prayer:

> *"Create in me a pure heart, O God, and renew a steadfast spirit within me."*
> **Psalm 51:10**

And remember the wisdom of Proverbs:

> *"One who has unreliable friends soon comes to ruin, but there is a friend who sticks closer than a brother."*
> **Proverbs 18:24**

Boundaries guard against bondage. Reset restores what was broken. Together, they open the way for freedom in Christ and prepare the soil for authentic, Christ-centered relationships.

CHAPTER 6
THE DIGITAL ADDICTION SELF-ASSESSMENT AND SPIRITUAL RESET

This chapter marks a turning point in our journey. Up to now, we have examined the dangers of social media, the spiritual warfare it creates, and the way sin, deviance, and brokenness manifest through it. Now it is time to pause and look inward with honesty. Scripture urges self-examination:

> *"Examine yourselves to see whether you are in the faith; test yourselves. Do you not realize that Christ Jesus is in you—unless, of course, you fail the test?"*
> **2 Corinthians 13:5**

The goal of this chapter is not condemnation but clarity. Many teens and families sense that something is off; the following pages help us name it, measure it, and begin the path back to freedom.

The assessment that follows is designed to surface the patterns of digital dependency that often hide beneath the surface. It does not reduce a person to a score; rather, it provides a mirror. Answer honestly. Then bring what you discover into the light of Christ.

The Digital Addiction Self-Assessment

Section 1: Behavioral Patterns

Rate each statement on a scale of 0–3:
0 = Never true
1 = Occasionally true
2 = Often true
3 = Almost always true

	I check my phone or social media accounts within 15 minutes of waking up.
	I feel anxious or uncomfortable when I can't access my phone or social media.
	I find myself checking social media at times when I intended to do other things.
	I have trouble maintaining focus on tasks without checking my devices.
	I spend more time on social media or digital devices than I initially planned.
	I've tried to reduce my screen time but found it difficult or impossible to maintain.
	I use my phone in bed before sleeping.
	I check my phone during meals with others.

	I interrupt in-person conversations to check notifications.
	I feel phantom vibrations or hear phantom notification sounds when my phone is off.
	Section 1: Behavioral Patterns Total

Section 2: Emotional Impact

Rate each statement on the same 0–3 scale:

	I feel a sense of emptiness or dissatisfaction after spending time on social media.
	I compare myself negatively to others based on their social media presence.
	My mood is affected by the response (or lack of) to my posts or messages.
	I feel anxious when unable to check notifications immediately.
	I experience FOMO (fear of missing out) when seeing others' activities online.
	I feel relief or pleasure when receiving notifications or messages.
	I feel irritable or restless when trying to reduce screen time.
	I use social media or digital content to escape uncomfortable emotions.
	I feel guilty about the amount of time I spend on digital devices.
	I feel less satisfied with my actual life after viewing idealized content online.

	Section 2: Emotional Impact Total

Section 3: Relational Impact

Rate each statement on the same 0–3 scale:

	People close to me have expressed concern about my digital habits.
	I've been physically present but mentally absent with loved ones due to device use.
	I've missed important moments because I was engaged with my device.
	I find in-person interactions less stimulating than online engagement.
	I communicate with friends more through devices than in person.
	I've experienced conflict in relationships due to my digital habits.
	I sometimes prefer interacting with people online rather than face-to-face.
	I've declined or avoided in-person social activities in favor of digital engagement.
	I find it difficult to be fully present in conversations without checking my device.
	I share significant life events on social media before telling close friends or family.
	Section 3: Relational Impact Total

Section 4: Spiritual Impact

Rate each statement on the same 0–3 scale:

	My digital habits interfere with spiritual practices like prayer or Scripture reading.
	I find it harder to experience silence or solitude due to digital distractions.
	I feel spiritually empty or disconnected after extended screen time.
	I turn to digital content rather than spiritual resources when feeling lost or confused.
	My sense of worth is influenced by online metrics (likes, followers, etc.).
	It is difficult to focus during church or gatherings without checking my device.
	I spend more time consuming digital content than engaging with spiritual practices.
	My digital consumption exposes me to content that contradicts my spiritual values.
	I feel God seems more distant after extended time online.
	I find myself measuring my spiritual life against others' online presentations.
	Section 4: Spiritual Impact Total

Scoring and Interpretation

Add your scores from all four sections for a total between 0 and 120.

Your Overall Assessment Total

0–30 indicates healthy digital engagement with good boundaries and minimal negative impact.

31–60 suggests mild digital dependency worth addressing before it deepens.

61–90 signals moderate digital addiction with emotional, relational, and spiritual consequences that call for structured boundaries and support.

91–120 reflects severe digital addiction with significant distress and dysfunction; professional support, in addition to the strategies in this book, may be necessary.

Beyond the Numbers: Qualitative Reflection

The number is a starting point. Deeper insight comes from noticing patterns. Which section is highest—behavioral, emotional, relational, or spiritual? Which individual statements received your strongest responses? Do you see contradictions between what you believe about your habits and what your behavior reveals? Are your patterns stable, worsening, or improving over time? Stand in the light of truth without fear. The aim is freedom, not shame.

The Spiritual Dimension of Digital Addiction

What distinguishes this assessment from secular tools is its attention to the spiritual. Digital addiction does not only alter behavior and mood; it impoverishes our capacity for transcendence, meaning, and communion with God. Jesus posed a piercing question that echoes in our age of constant connection:

> *"What good is it for someone to gain the whole world, yet forfeit their soul?"*
> **Mark 8:36**

Our generation can gain unlimited digital access and still lose the capacity for presence, wonder, and authentic relationship.

Many teens and parents discover that their worth has been quietly pegged to metrics and feedback loops. The heart's restlessness is real. As Augustine confessed, our hearts are restless until they rest in God. Social platforms monetize that restlessness; they rarely satisfy it. The soul is the battleground between the cravings of the body and the call of the spirit, and every alert or like can tug the heart toward false worship.

Rewiring Neural Pathways

When Sarah, a college sophomore, chose to reduce her social media use, she felt what she called withdrawal. Her hand reached for the phone without conscious thought; irritability and emptiness followed. This is more than a habit; it is a neurological pattern. Dopamine—the brain's messenger for reward, learning, and motivation—releases with every novel stimulus, every unpredictable "win." Social platforms are built on variable reward schedules: you refresh, you might receive a like, a comment, a message, or nothing at all. That maybe is the hook.

Neuroscience explains why teens are especially vulnerable. The prefrontal cortex—the brain's center for impulse control and future-oriented decision-making—matures into the mid-to-late twenties. This developmental window means adolescents feel rewards more intensely and find it harder to resist them. In practice, a single viral post can condition a teen to chase the next high through constant checking and posting, even at the cost of sleep, school, or spiritual life. Author and psychiatrist Anna Lembke has described the smartphone as a delivery device for "digital dopamine," highlighting how continuous access to reward signals can create compulsive loops if left unchecked. (National Institute of Mental Health, PMC, Goodreads)

The data align with lived reality. National polling has estimated U.S. teens spend nearly five hours per day on social media, with many surpassing that threshold. Prolonged nightly use often displaces sleep, and public health surveillance continues to warn that a large majority of high school students get less than the recommended amount of sleep, with downstream effects on mental and physical health. These are not isolated anecdotes but patterns shaping a generation's attention, emotions, and choices. (Gallup.com, CDC)

Yet hope is real because the brain is plastic; pathways that were trained by compulsion can be retrained by wisdom, community, and grace. What science calls neuroplasticity, Scripture calls renewing the mind. The God who formed our inward parts also restores them.

From Assessment to Action

Self-knowledge becomes transformation when it is brought to Christ and practiced in community. Isolation strengthens addiction; truth-telling weakens it. Share your honest results with a trusted mentor or parent. Identify one pattern to address now, not later. Schedule a follow-up assessment in thirty days to track change. Remember that the goal is not digital asceticism but digital wisdom: to integrate technology in ways that serve, rather than sabotage, a life of love for God and neighbor.

Spiritual Reset After the Assessment

The assessment is not the end; it is the doorway. The way forward is a spiritual reset—three movements that carry us from bondage to freedom: repentance, renewal, and reorientation.

Repentance

Repentance is not self-condemnation; it is a turning. It begins when we name our sin plainly: we have let screens, metrics, and the approval of others occupy the throne of our hearts. Peter proclaimed,

> *"Repent, then, and turn to God, so that your sins may be wiped out, that times of refreshing may come from the Lord"*
> **Acts 3:19**

In biblical terms, repentance is a gift, not a punishment. It clears the fog of denial and lets the wind of God's mercy blow through the soul. Theologically, repentance reorders love: we dethrone false gods and enthrone Christ again.

Renewal

Renewal transforms what we love and how we think. Paul exhorts,

> *"Do not conform to the pattern of this world, but be transformed by the renewing of your mind"*
> **Romans 12:2**

Conformity is the algorithm we live in without noticing; renewal is the Spirit's work as we saturate our minds with Scripture and prayer. The psalmist testifies,

> *"The law of the Lord is perfect, refreshing the soul. The statutes of the Lord are trustworthy, making wise the simple"*
> **Psalm 19:7**

Renewal replaces comparison with contentment, frenzy with peace, and noise with the knowledge of God.

Reorientation

Reorientation is the fixed gaze that follows renewal. Hebrews urges,

> *"Let us run with perseverance the race marked out for us, fixing our eyes on Jesus, the pioneer and perfecter of faith"*
> **Hebrews 12:1–2**

Practically, reorientation means we reshape our days around God's presence and mission. We reclaim mornings for unhurried prayer and Scripture before our eyes touch a screen. We restructure evenings so sleep is protected. We prioritize worship and embodied community over digital drift. Reorientation is not merely saying no to devices; it is saying yes to the abundant life Jesus promised.

Strategies for Breaking Digital Strongholds

Pattern Interruption

One of the first ways to break digital addiction is to interrupt the automatic patterns that have been carved into the brain. Over time, the simple act of reaching for a phone at every pause in conversation or boredom moment becomes nearly unconscious. This is how sin often works: habits form grooves that steer us without thought.

A teen named Daniel confessed that he no longer chose to check his phone—his hand simply moved on its own. To fight back, he placed a small sticker on the back of his phone case with the words: "Is this necessary?" That question, seen at the critical moment, slowed his reflex and created space to make a choice.

Scripture calls this

> *"taking every thought captive to make it obedient to Christ"*
> **2 Corinthians 10:5**

Pattern interruption is both neurological and spiritual. It is disrupting the groove that sin has made in the mind so that the Spirit may re-train it for holiness.

Dopamine Fasting

Science has shown that one reason social media feels so addictive is because of dopamine—the brain's reward chemical. Every notification delivers a small hit of pleasure. But the real hook is unpredictability: not every refresh brings a reward, so we keep refreshing in hope. Psychologists call this variable reward scheduling, and it is one of the strongest drivers of compulsive behavior.

Dr. Anna Lembke of Stanford has called smartphones "the hypodermic needle that delivers digital dopamine 24/7." The constant stimulation eventually exhausts the brain's receptors, leaving users restless and unsatisfied with ordinary life. The Bible already understood the wisdom of fasting. Jesus declared,

> *"When you fast, do not look somber as the hypocrites do, for they disfigure their faces to show others they are fasting. Truly I tell you, they have received their reward in full. But when you fast, put oil on your head and wash your face, so that it will not be obvious to others that you are fasting, but only to your Father, who is unseen; and your Father, who sees what is done in secret, will reward you"*
> ***Matthew 6:16–18***

A digital fast functions the same way. By abstaining from screens for set times—whether an hour before bed, a full Sunday Sabbath, or a weeklong break—dopamine levels rebalance, and the soul finds clarity. A youth group in Ohio began practicing "No-Phone Sundays," and within weeks, teens testified that they felt calmer, slept better, and enjoyed meals more deeply. The fasting created hunger for real presence.

Replacement Behaviors

Jesus taught that casting out one spirit without filling the void can be dangerous:

> *"When an impure spirit comes out of a person, it goes through arid places seeking rest and does not find it. Then it says, 'I will return to the house I left.' When it arrives, it finds the house swept clean and put in order. Then it goes and takes seven other spirits more wicked than itself, and they go in and live there. And the final condition of that person is worse than the first"*
> **Luke 11:24–26**

The same is true for digital habits. Simply deleting an app without replacing it with healthier practices leaves the vacuum empty and vulnerable. Teens who remove TikTok but do not replace it with meaningful activities often relapse quickly.

Instead, new pathways must be created. A student named Emily shared that she replaced her nightly scrolling with journaling prayers. At first, it felt dry. But within a month, she reported deeper sleep, more gratitude, and an increasing sense of God's presence. Replacement is not deprivation—it is restoration.

Attention Training

One of the greatest casualties of digital life is attention. Teens raised in the constant flicker of notifications often struggle to concentrate even for minutes at a time. Yet God has called His people to sustained attention—on Him, His Word, and one another.

Students in one Christian college were challenged to begin with five minutes of silent prayer each morning. At first, it felt impossible; their minds scattered in every direction. But over weeks, they found their capacity for worship, study, and even conversation expanding.

Paul's words come alive here:

> *"Set your minds on things above, not on earthly things"*
> **Colossians 3:2**

Training the mind to focus is a spiritual discipline, and every reclaimed minute of undivided attention is a victory against the culture of distraction.

Conscious Consumption

Not all digital use is evil. Social media can connect, encourage, and even spread the gospel. But too often, we use it reactively, without thought. Conscious consumption means deciding why, when, and how to engage before opening an app.

A mother of three created a family rule: "No social media without purpose." Each teen had to articulate why they were logging in—whether to check on a friend, message someone, or post something uplifting. Mindless scrolling was not permitted. Within months, the family reported more peace and fewer conflicts.

Paul's words ring true:

> *"I have the right to do anything," you say—but not everything is beneficial. "I have the right to do anything"—but I will not be mastered by anything*
> **1 Corinthians 6:12**

Conscious consumption breaks mastery by restoring intentionality.

Community Reinforcement

Addiction thrives in isolation but heals in community. Teens fighting digital dependency often fail alone but flourish when supported by peers, parents, and church family.

A youth pastor in Texas introduced "Phones-Away Fridays" where students left devices at the church door and engaged in games, worship, and fellowship. The change was dramatic: teens began to look forward to real connection, discovering joy in being fully present.

Hebrews exhorts us:

> *"And let us consider how we may spur one another on toward love and good deeds, not giving up meeting together, as some are in the habit of doing, but encouraging one another"*
> **Hebrews 10:24–25**

Digital freedom is rarely won in isolation; it blossoms in authentic, embodied community.

Addiction's Toll on Body, Soul, and Spirit

Digital addiction corrodes us on every level of our created nature. Scripture affirms that human beings are three-part creations—body, soul, and spirit. Paul prayed,

> *"May God himself, the God of peace, sanctify you through and through. May your whole spirit, soul and body be kept blameless at the coming of our Lord Jesus Christ"*
> **1 Thessalonians 5:23)**

Addiction disrupts this harmony.

The body is weakened. Teens immersed in late-night scrolling often experience sleep deprivation, weight fluctuation, headaches, and chronic fatigue. Research from the CDC reports that over 70% of high school students fail to achieve the recommended hours of sleep, and increased screen time is one of the leading causes. Lack of sleep affects memory, emotional regulation, and physical health, leaving the body restless and anxious.

The soul—the seat of mind, will, and emotions—is fractured. Constant comparison breeds envy, likes become the measure of worth, and the will weakens under the burden of compulsive checking. The DOJ has noted correlations between high social media use and increases in youth delinquency and deviance, particularly bullying and sexual misconduct, which are rooted in disordered emotions and choices. When the soul is enslaved, peace is replaced with turmoil.

The spirit—the deepest part of us made for communion with God—grows silent. Prayer is crowded out by posts. Worship becomes distracted. Time with God competes against time online, and the spirit starves. Jesus warned,

> *"When your eyes are healthy, your whole body also is full of light. But when they are unhealthy, your body also is full of darkness"*
> **Luke 11:34**

Addiction blinds the eyes of the spirit, leaving darkness where there should be light.

The Importance of Boundaries

Breaking addiction requires boundaries. These are not chains but fences that protect freedom. The Psalmist wrote,

> *"The boundary lines have fallen for me in pleasant places; surely I have a delightful inheritance"*
> **Psalm 16:6**

For teens, boundaries may include: limiting social media to one or two daily check-ins, setting devices aside an hour before bed, or even reducing online "friends." Proverbs warns,

> *"One who has unreliable friends soon comes to ruin, but there is a friend who sticks closer than a brother"*
> **Proverbs 18:24**

Teens with hundreds or thousands of online connections often discover that very few are genuine. By setting boundaries on the number of digital friends and the time invested, they learn to value authentic relationships rooted in Christ and family.

A story illustrates this truth. Jake, a 16-year-old, had over 1,500 followers but felt increasingly lonely. He began a practice of "digital pruning," keeping only those he knew in real life and trusted. At first, the emptiness felt deeper. But over time, the noise diminished, and his true friendships deepened. With less distraction, Jake began to enjoy meals with his parents and even volunteered at his church youth group. His story shows that boundaries are not subtraction—they are restoration.

Spiritual Reset After the Assessment

Spiritual reset which interchangeably equates her to "digital resets" requires not only boundaries but repentance, renewal, and reorientation, as described earlier. To live this out, practical disciplines are needed. Repentance is expressed not just in words but in turning away from sin. Renewal is pursued through consistent engagement with Scripture. Reorientation is practiced by fixing the eyes daily on Christ, sometimes with the simple prayer of Psalm 27:1: "The Lord is my light and my salvation—whom shall I fear? The Lord is the stronghold of my life—of whom shall I be afraid?"

Digital resets can include a multitude of intentional activities but a few that have proven to at least initiate a spiritual reset include a weekly "tech Sabbath," where all devices are laid aside from sundown to sundown, a daily morning routine where Scripture is read before any device is opened, and a nightly prayer in place of scrolling, restoring peace to the mind and spirit before sleep.

Chapter 6 Reflection

Pause for a moment now. Consider your assessment responses. What habits enslave you most? Where do you sense your body is weary, your soul fractured, or your spirit silenced? Confess these before God in prayer.

Pray aloud David's cry: "Create in me a pure heart, O God, and renew a steadfast spirit within me" (Psalm 51:10).

Ask Him to show you one boundary to set this week. It may be as simple as charging your phone outside your bedroom, committing to device-free dinners, or pruning your online friendships. Small steps open the door to great freedom.

Remember, Christ has already won the victory.

> *"So if the Son sets you free, you will be free indeed"*
> **John 8:36**

CHAPTER 7
BREAKING FREE: THE POWER OF CONFESSION AND ACCOUNTABILITY

Freedom is not found in isolation. Addiction thrives in secrecy, but healing begins when we bring our struggles into the light. John writes,

> *"If we confess our sins, he is faithful and just and will forgive us our sins and purify us from all unrighteousness"*
> **1 John 1:9**

Confession is not a punishment; it is the doorway to freedom.

The Power of Confession

Sin loses power when it is named. Social media addiction, like any bondage, tightens its grip when hidden in shame. Satan thrives in secrecy, whispering lies that no one will understand, that we are beyond hope, or that the sin is too small to matter. But the Word of God tells us otherwise:

> *"Therefore confess your sins to each other and pray for each other so that you may be healed. The prayer of a righteous person is powerful and effective"*
> ***James 5:16***

Healing comes not through hiding but through honesty before God and trusted believers.

Confession aligns us with truth. It strips away denial and forces us to see ourselves clearly in the light of God's holiness. David knew this firsthand:

> *"When I kept silent, my bones wasted away through my groaning all day long. For day and night your hand was heavy on me; my strength was sapped as in the heat of summer. Then I acknowledged my sin to you and did not cover up my iniquity. I said, 'I will confess my transgressions to the Lord.' And you forgave the guilt of my sin"*
> ***Psalm 32:3–5***

What secrecy destroys, confession restores.

One teen named Caleb described his addiction to late-night scrolling and pornography as "chains he could not break." For months he told himself he would stop, but nothing changed. When he finally confessed to his youth pastor, he was shocked to find compassion instead of condemnation. Together they prayed, set accountability measures, and tracked his progress.

Caleb later said, "The moment I confessed, it felt like Satan's lie of isolation shattered." Confession, he discovered, was not the end of his dignity but the beginning of his deliverance.

The Gift of Accountability

Confession is the beginning, but accountability sustains the journey. Solomon observed,

> *"Though one may be overpowered, two can defend themselves. A cord of three strands is not quickly broken"*
> **Ecclesiastes 4:12**

We were never meant to fight alone.

Accountability provides encouragement when we are weak, correction when we stray, and celebration when we succeed. For a teen struggling with late-night scrolling, an accountability partner might be a parent who collects the phone before bedtime, or a friend who checks in with encouragement and prayer. For parents, it may mean honest conversations with other believers about family media habits. For churches, it means creating safe spaces where confession is met with grace, not judgment.

The early church practiced accountability in community. Acts 2:42 tells us,

> *"They devoted themselves to the apostles' teaching and to fellowship, to the breaking of bread and to prayer."*
> **Acts 2:42**

Their unity provided strength against temptation and courage against persecution. Likewise, when teens walk in community, they find strength against digital temptations.

Renewal of the Mind

Confession and accountability are only part of the picture. For lasting freedom, there must be renewal of the mind. Paul wrote,

> *"Do not conform to the pattern of this world, but be transformed by the renewing of your mind. Then you will be able to test and approve what God's will is—his good, pleasing and perfect will"*
> **Romans 12:2**

Renewal is not behavior modification; it is the transformation of thought, belief, and desire at the deepest level.

Paul also writes,

> *"In your relationships with one another, have the same mindset as Christ Jesus: Who, being in very nature God, did not consider equality with God something to be used to his own advantage; rather, he made himself nothing by taking the very nature of a servant, being made in human likeness"*
> **Philippians 2:5–7**

To put on the mind of Christ is to reject the self-centeredness that social media encourages and embrace humility, service, and truth.

A teen named Amber confessed that she found herself scrolling endlessly, comparing her looks to influencers online. Her mind was filled with envy and self-hatred. But through discipleship, she began memorizing Scriptures about her identity in Christ. Slowly, her perspective shifted. "I realized," she said, "that I don't have to compete for likes because Jesus already calls me beloved." Renewal of the mind gave her freedom from the slavery of comparison.

Renewal is critical because social media thrives on patterns of this world: vanity, consumerism, outrage, and lust. Paul warns of what this world will look like in the last days:

> *"But mark this: There will be terrible times in the last days. People will be lovers of themselves, lovers of money, boastful, proud, abusive, disobedient to their parents, ungrateful, unholy, without love, unforgiving, slanderous, without self-control, brutal, not lovers of the good, treacherous, rash, conceited, lovers of pleasure rather than lovers of God—having a form of godliness but denying its power. Have nothing to do with such people"*
> **2 Timothy 3:1–5**

Social media, for many teens, accelerates these traits. Selfies and curated feeds fuel self-love and pride. Influencer culture glamorizes money and materialism. Cancel culture stokes abuse and slander. Anonymous posting erodes self-control. What Paul described nearly two thousand years ago is now on display daily through digital platforms.

Mental Health in the Digital Age

Renewing the mind is particularly urgent in light of the mental health crisis among teens. The CDC reports that 42% of high school students in the United States felt persistently sad or hopeless in 2021, a significant increase from previous decades. Social media is a major contributing factor. It fuels anxiety through fear of missing out, creates depression through constant comparison, and intensifies loneliness by replacing authentic relationships with shallow interactions.

Psychologists have identified links between social media use and increased incidents of depression, self-harm, and suicide among adolescents. The National Institute of Mental Health has warned that adolescents who spend more than three hours a day on social media are more likely to experience symptoms of anxiety and depression. Given that Pew Research shows nearly half of U.S. teens are online "almost constantly," the implications are alarming.

One teen, Emily, shared that every time she posted a picture, she anxiously waited for likes and comments. If they came slowly, she felt worthless. If a friend received more attention, jealousy consumed her. Eventually, she admitted, "I stopped enjoying life. I was only living for what people thought of me online." Emily's story reflects what countless teens face: their sense of identity is shaped not by God's truth but by the fleeting applause of digital crowds.

The Bible points to a different foundation. Paul urges,

> *"Set your minds on things above, not on earthly things"*
> **Colossians 3:2**

Renewal of the mind means lifting our focus from likes and notifications to the eternal truth of God's love.

Body, Soul, and Spirit Renewal

Addiction and deviance fracture the person. Only Christ can restore wholeness to body, soul, and spirit.

The body suffers under digital addiction. Late nights scrolling leave teens exhausted, with weakened immune systems and impaired learning. Research from the American Academy of Pediatrics shows that teens who use screens excessively before bed have significantly poorer sleep quality and increased risk of obesity. Renewal of the body begins with rest. God established rhythms of Sabbath not to burden us but to restore us:

> *"By the seventh day God had finished the work he had been doing; so on the seventh day he rested from all his work"*
> **Genesis 2:2**

A teen who sets down the phone and chooses rest steps into God's pattern of renewal.

The soul—the mind, will, and emotions—bears the deepest scars of digital sin. Lies whispered online create shame, envy, and despair. But God's Word renews the soul. David declared,

> *"The law of the Lord is perfect, refreshing the soul. The statutes of the Lord are trustworthy, making wise the simple"*
> ***Psalm 19:7***

Renewal of the soul happens as truth replaces lies, peace replaces anxiety, and hope replaces despair.

The spirit is the place of communion with God, and it is often the most neglected. Social media promises connection but leaves the spirit starving. Jesus warned,

> *"Man shall not live on bread alone, but on every word that comes from the mouth of God"*
> ***Matthew 4:4***

When teens turn from constant scrolling to prayer, Scripture, and worship, the spirit awakens to God's presence.

Paul explains this transformation in 2 Corinthians 5:17:

> *"Therefore, if anyone is in Christ, the new creation has come: The old has gone, the new is here!"*
> ***2 Corinthians 5:17***

Renewal in Christ is not partial. It is total. The body, soul, and spirit are all invited into wholeness. A teen once trapped in addiction can truly say, "I am not who I was—I am new."

Biblical Parallels of Renewal

The Bible is full of stories of people whose lives were fractured by sin yet renewed by God. Consider

> *"Set your minds on things above, not on earthly things"*
> **Colossians 3:2**

Renewal of the mind means lifting our focus from likes and notifications to the eternal truth of God's love.

Body, Soul, and Spirit Renewal

Addiction and deviance fracture the person. Only Christ can restore wholeness to body, soul, and spirit.

The body suffers under digital addiction. Late nights scrolling leave teens exhausted, with weakened immune systems and impaired learning. Research from the American Academy of Pediatrics shows that teens who use screens excessively before bed have significantly poorer sleep quality and increased risk of obesity. Renewal of the body begins with rest. God established rhythms of Sabbath not to burden us but to restore us:

> *"By the seventh day God had finished the work he had been doing; so on the seventh day he rested from all his work"*
> **Genesis 2:2**

A teen who sets down the phone and chooses rest steps into God's pattern of renewal.

The soul—the mind, will, and emotions—bears the deepest scars of digital sin. Lies whispered online create shame, envy, and despair. But God's Word renews the soul. David declared,

> *"The law of the Lord is perfect, refreshing the soul. The statutes of the Lord are trustworthy, making wise the simple"*
> **Psalm 19:7**

Renewal of the soul happens as truth replaces lies, peace replaces anxiety, and hope replaces despair.

The spirit is the place of communion with God, and it is often the most neglected. Social media promises connection but leaves the spirit starving. Jesus warned,

> *"Man shall not live on bread alone, but on every word that comes from the mouth of God"*
> **Matthew 4:4**

When teens turn from constant scrolling to prayer, Scripture, and worship, the spirit awakens to God's presence.

Paul explains this transformation in 2 Corinthians 5:17:

> *"Therefore, if anyone is in Christ, the new creation has come: The old has gone, the new is here!"*
> **2 Corinthians 5:17**

Renewal in Christ is not partial. It is total. The body, soul, and spirit are all invited into wholeness. A teen once trapped in addiction can truly say, "I am not who I was—I am new."

Biblical Parallels of Renewal

The Bible is full of stories of people whose lives were fractured by sin yet renewed by God. Consider

> *"Set your minds on things above, not on earthly things"*
> **Colossians 3:2**

Renewal of the mind means lifting our focus from likes and notifications to the eternal truth of God's love.

Body, Soul, and Spirit Renewal

Addiction and deviance fracture the person. Only Christ can restore wholeness to body, soul, and spirit.

The body suffers under digital addiction. Late nights scrolling leave teens exhausted, with weakened immune systems and impaired learning. Research from the American Academy of Pediatrics shows that teens who use screens excessively before bed have significantly poorer sleep quality and increased risk of obesity. Renewal of the body begins with rest. God established rhythms of Sabbath not to burden us but to restore us:

> *"By the seventh day God had finished the work he had been doing; so on the seventh day he rested from all his work"*
> **Genesis 2:2**

A teen who sets down the phone and chooses rest steps into God's pattern of renewal.

The soul—the mind, will, and emotions—bears the deepest scars of digital sin. Lies whispered online create shame, envy, and despair. But God's Word renews the soul. David declared,

> *"The law of the Lord is perfect, refreshing the soul. The statutes of the Lord are trustworthy, making wise the simple"*
> **Psalm 19:7**

Renewal of the soul happens as truth replaces lies, peace replaces anxiety, and hope replaces despair.

The spirit is the place of communion with God, and it is often the most neglected. Social media promises connection but leaves the spirit starving. Jesus warned,

> *"Man shall not live on bread alone, but on every word that comes from the mouth of God"*
> **Matthew 4:4**

When teens turn from constant scrolling to prayer, Scripture, and worship, the spirit awakens to God's presence.

Paul explains this transformation in 2 Corinthians 5:17:

> *"Therefore, if anyone is in Christ, the new creation has come: The old has gone, the new is here!"*
> **2 Corinthians 5:17**

Renewal in Christ is not partial. It is total. The body, soul, and spirit are all invited into wholeness. A teen once trapped in addiction can truly say, "I am not who I was—I am new."

Biblical Parallels of Renewal

The Bible is full of stories of people whose lives were fractured by sin yet renewed by God. Consider

Peter. After denying Jesus three times, he was crushed by shame. His mind was clouded with fear, his soul broken with guilt, and his spirit silenced. Yet after the resurrection, Jesus restored him. Three times Jesus asked, "Do you love me?" and three times Peter confessed his devotion. His renewal was complete, and he became a bold preacher at Pentecost, leading thousands to Christ. Peter's story mirrors the truth for teens today: no matter the depth of failure, Christ renews completely.

Another example is the demoniac of the Gerasenes in Mark 5. He lived in isolation, broken in body, tormented in soul, enslaved in spirit. When Jesus delivered him, the people found him

> *"...sitting there, dressed and in his right mind"*
> **Mark 5:15**

Body, soul, and spirit were restored by the power of Christ. Teens trapped in digital bondage can likewise experience freedom that brings clarity, peace, and communion with God.

A Story of Renewal

Michael, a seventeen-year-old, confessed that his life revolved around social media. He admitted spending nearly ten hours a day online, often at the expense of homework, sleep, and prayer. "I felt empty," he said, "like nothing mattered except the next notification." After confessing to his parents and youth leader, he began a journey of accountability. They helped him set boundaries, but more importantly, they pointed him to Scripture. Michael memorized 2 Corinthians 5:17 and repeated it daily. Slowly, his habits changed. He regained sleep, his grades improved, and he started leading worship at his church. Michael said, "I didn't just delete apps. God renewed me."

Chapter 7 Reflection

Where do you need renewal? Is it in your body—your sleep, your health, your rhythms of rest? Is it in your soul—your thought life, your emotions, your will? Or is it in your spirit—your connection with God? Confess honestly. Bring it into the light with God and with someone you trust.

Pray this prayer from Romans 12:2:

> *"Do not conform to the pattern of this world, but be transformed by the renewing of your mind. Then you will be able to test and approve what God's will is—his good, pleasing and perfect will."*
> **Romans 12:2**

Confession is not weakness; it is strength. Accountability is not restriction; it is freedom. Renewal is not impossible; it is promised in Christ. He who made all things new will make you new as well.

CHAPTER 8
RENEWING THE MIND THROUGH GOD'S WORD

Social media disciples the mind daily. Every post, image, and video teaches something about identity, worth, and truth. Paul warns,

> *"Do not conform to the pattern of this world, but be transformed by the renewing of your mind. Then you will be able to test and approve what God's will is—his good, pleasing and perfect will"*
> **Romans 12:2**

The only antidote to digital lies is divine truth.

The Pattern of This World

The pattern of social media is comparison, performance, and distraction. Teens measure themselves by likes, followers, and comments. Their value becomes tied to digital applause. This is nothing new. Paul described the same cycle in his day:

> *"They exchanged the truth about God for a lie, and worshiped and served created things rather than the Creator—who is forever praised. Amen"*
> **Romans 1:25**

Social media is simply a new form of an old problem: idolatry of the created over the Creator.

Paul warned Timothy that in the last days, people would be

> *"lovers of themselves, lovers of money, boastful, proud, abusive, disobedient to their parents, ungrateful, unholy, without love, unforgiving, slanderous, without self-control, brutal, not lovers of the good, treacherous, rash, conceited, lovers of pleasure rather than lovers of God—having a form of godliness but denying its power"*
> **2 Timothy 3:2–5**

These very traits are not just creeping into society—they are being celebrated on social media. The "pattern of this world" is now visible in every feed.

A teen named Jason admitted, "Every time I opened TikTok, I felt like I had to keep up. The guys I followed were showing off cars, money, girls, and status. I thought if I didn't have that, I was nothing." Jason's thinking mirrored the world, not Christ. Left unchallenged, these patterns pull the soul deeper into bondage.

The Battlefield of the Mind

Scripture teaches that the mind is the control center of life.

> *"For as he thinks in his heart, so is he"*
> **Proverbs 23:7**

Whatever dominates the thoughts eventually shapes the actions, and whatever shapes the actions defines the destiny. This is why the mind is Satan's primary battlefield.

Joyce Meyer's Battlefield of the Mind emphasizes that every stronghold begins with a thought. Social media is designed to plant and reinforce thoughts—thoughts of inadequacy, of envy, of lust, of rage. Left unchallenged, these thoughts grow into behaviors and habits. The soul—the seat of the mind, will, and emotions—becomes a battleground between the flesh enticed by the ruler of this world and the spirit longing for God.

Paul urges us to think differently:

> *"Do nothing out of selfish ambition or vain conceit. Rather, in humility value others above yourselves, not looking to your own interests but each of you to the interests of the others"*
> **Philippians 2:3–4**

Social media pushes selfish ambition, but the renewed mind chooses humility.

Walking in the Spirit

The battle is not fought in human strength alone. Paul writes,

> *"So I say, walk by the Spirit, and you will not gratify the desires of the flesh"*
> **Galatians 5:16**

Likewise,

> *"For those who are led by the Spirit of God are the children of God"*
> **Romans 8:14**

To walk in the Spirit means to submit daily to God's direction, to let His Word and His Spirit govern thoughts, words, and actions.

Jesus Himself warned,

> *"The thief comes only to steal and kill and destroy; I have come that they may have life, and have it to the full"*
> **John 10:10**

Social media may promise connection, entertainment, or recognition, but beneath the surface, it often steals time, kills joy, and destroys identity. The renewed mind recognizes the thief and resists him. James exhorts,

> *"Submit yourselves, then, to God. Resist the devil, and he will flee from you"*
> **James 4:7**

A teen named Maya struggled with self-harm, fueled by online communities that glorified pain. Her breakthrough came when she replaced those voices with daily reading in Psalms.

> *"I started with Psalm 139, where it says, 'I praise you because I am fearfully and wonderfully made'*
> **Psalm 139:14**

I wrote it on my mirror. Every time the old thoughts came, I read it aloud." Over time, she walked in the Spirit by rejecting the lies and replacing them with truth. Her testimony was one of survival through surrender.

Renewal of the Mind Through Scripture

The renewal Paul speaks of is not superficial. It is not simply replacing bad habits with better ones. It is a radical reorientation of thought, desire, and purpose. Paul teaches,

> *"For the word of God is alive and active. Sharper than any double-edged sword, it penetrates even to dividing soul and spirit, joints and marrow; it judges the thoughts and attitudes of the heart"*
> **Hebrews 4:12**

God's Word exposes the lies, cuts away the falsehood, and implants truth deep into the soul.

This is why daily Scripture is essential. Teens who replace even fifteen minutes of scrolling with fifteen minutes of Bible reading discover a new voice shaping their thoughts. Parents who read Scripture aloud at the dinner table find their children absorbing truth that counters the world's lies. Churches that prioritize teaching the Word equip their members with the only weapon that can withstand deception: the sword of the Spirit.

Proverbs 23:7 reminds us that

> *"as he thinks in his heart, so is he."*
> **Proverbs 23:7**

The mind dictates the man. A renewed mind in Christ leads to a renewed life in Christ. This is why Paul insists we

> *"take captive every thought to make it obedient to Christ"*
> **2 Corinthians 10:5**

Every negative comparison, every lustful image, every envious thought presented on social media must be captured and surrendered to God's truth.

Body, Soul, and Spirit in Renewal

Social media addiction attacks the whole person, but God's Word restores wholeness. The body benefits when rhythms of rest are supported by rhythms of Scripture. Research shows that teens who disengage from digital media before bed experience better sleep, reduced stress, and improved health outcomes (American Academy of Pediatrics, 2016). When phones are set aside and Scripture is read, the body is calmed by God's peace.

> *"In peace I will lie down and sleep, for you alone, Lord, make me dwell in safety"*
> **Psalm 4:8**

The soul—the mind, will, and emotions—is renewed as it is filled with God's truth. Anxiety is replaced with peace, despair with hope, envy with gratitude. Romans 8:6 teaches,

> *"The mind governed by the flesh is death, but the mind governed by the Spirit is life and peace."*
> **Romans 8:6**

When teens learn to govern their thoughts with Scripture, the soul is fortified against the storm of digital lies.

The spirit thrives as communion with God deepens through His living Word. Jesus declared,

> *"Man shall not live on bread alone, but on every word that comes from the mouth of God"*
> **Matthew 4:4**

The Word nourishes the spirit. A teen whose spirit is well-fed in prayer and Scripture will be far less vulnerable to the false promises of social media.

Paul proclaims the fullness of this renewal:

> *"Therefore, if anyone is in Christ, the new creation has come: The old has gone, the new is here!"*
> **2 Corinthians 5:17**

To walk in newness means the body is strengthened, the soul is stabilized, and the spirit is awakened.

The whole person is transformed into the likeness of Christ.

Biblical and Modern Parallels

The transformation of the mind is vividly illustrated in Scripture. Consider Paul himself. Once, his mind was filled with murderous hatred toward Christians. But after his encounter with Christ, his mind was renewed. He later wrote,

> *"For to me, to live is Christ and to die is gain"*
> **Philippians 1:21**

The persecutor became the preacher because his mind was reshaped by the truth of God's Word.

For a modern teen example, consider Liam, a high school sophomore. Consumed by Instagram, he admitted he was addicted to likes and validation. He later described his life as "a roller coaster based on other people's approval." But when his youth group challenged him to memorize Romans 12:2, he began replacing old patterns with daily Scripture reading. "It felt awkward at first," Liam said, "but the more I read, the less I cared about the likes. My confidence came from God's Word, not from people's comments."

The Enemy's Tactics and God's Victory

Jesus warned plainly:

> *"The thief comes only to steal and kill and destroy; I have come that they may have life, and have it to the full"*
> **John 10:10**

Social media, though not evil in itself, is often twisted by the thief. It steals joy, kills self-worth, and destroys peace. Yet Jesus promises abundant life—a life filled with truth, purpose, and freedom.

James 4:7 provides the posture of victory:

> *"Submit yourselves, then, to God. Resist the devil, and he will flee from you."*
> **James 4:7**

Teens who fill their minds with Scripture are not helpless. They are armed with truth. When the enemy whispers lies—"You are worthless," "No one cares about you," "You will never be enough"—they can answer with God's Word, just as Jesus did when tempted in the wilderness.

Chapter 8 Reflection

What thoughts have dominated your mind lately? Are they shaped more by the endless scroll of social media or by the eternal Word of God? Your mind will always be discipled by something. Which will it be—culture or Christ?

Pray this prayer from Psalm 119:

> *"I have hidden your word in my heart that I might not sin against you"*
> **Psalm 119:11**

Renewal is not a one-time act but a daily practice. The battle for the mind is fierce, but victory comes as the Word takes root and transforms us from the inside out. The soul is indeed a battlefield, but Christ is the Captain who leads us to triumph.

CHAPTER 9
THE 40-DAY SOCIAL MEDIA FREEDOM PLAN

The Significance of Forty

Throughout Scripture, the number forty represents seasons of testing, purification, preparation, and transformation. When God judged the earth, He caused rain to fall for forty days and nights to cleanse it of corruption:

> *"For forty days the flood kept coming on the earth, and as the waters increased they lifted the ark high above the earth"*
> ***Genesis 7:17***

When Moses ascended Mount Sinai, he spent forty days and nights in God's presence, receiving the Law (Exodus 24:18). Elijah journeyed forty days through the wilderness to encounter God at Mount Horeb (1 Kings

19:8). Jesus Himself fasted for forty days in the wilderness, resisting Satan's temptations by clinging to the Word of God (Matthew 4:1–11).

In each of these examples, forty marked a sacred period of cleansing and renewal. It was never about numbers alone but about God reshaping His people for His purposes. In the same way, this 40-Day Social Media Freedom Plan is not simply about giving up screen time — it is about purification, restoration, and transformation of the whole person: body, soul, and spirit.

A Spiritual Detox

Think of this as a spiritual detox. Social media, when consumed without wisdom, becomes toxic to the soul. It poisons identity through comparison, clouds judgment through lies, and corrupts desires through lust, greed, and envy. It steals time, drains peace, and breeds deviant behavior. Just as the flood waters cleansed the earth of its corruption, this forty-day journey invites you to let God wash away the toxins of digital bondage and restore you to freedom in Christ.

Paul reminds us,

> *"Do not conform to the pattern of this world, but be transformed by the renewing of your mind. Then you will be able to test and approve what God's will is — his good, pleasing and perfect will"*
> **Romans 12:2**

The transformation of the mind is the heart of this journey.

Accepting the Challenge

The Christian life is not passive. It requires resolve. Scripture calls us to rise up to challenges, not shrink back. Joshua was told,

> *"Be strong and courageous. Do not be afraid; do not be discouraged, for the Lord your God will be with you wherever you go"*
> **Joshua 1:9**

Paul exhorts,

> *"Run in such a way as to get the prize"*
> **1 Corinthians 9:24**

To embrace this plan is to accept a spiritual challenge — to step out of comfort, confront temptation, and pursue holiness.

Teens, parents, and church leaders: will you take the challenge? Will you commit to forty days of detox from the toxins of social media and feast instead on the Word of God? Victory is possible. Freedom is promised. The Son Himself has said:

> *"So if the Son sets you free, you will be free indeed"*
> **John 8:36**

Days 1–10: Awakening the Soul

Day 1: The Lord Is My Light

Scripture

> *"The Lord is my light and my salvation — whom shall I fear? The Lord is the stronghold of my life — of whom shall I be afraid?"*
> **Psalm 27:1**

Lesson

The first step to freedom is recognizing that God alone is our light. Social media pretends to offer light through constant updates and approval, but its glow is false. True security and strength come only from the Lord.

Reflection Questions
1. What fears driveme to pick up my phone so often?
2. Where am I looking for strength other than God?

Action Step

Write down your daily average screen time. Place it before God in prayer, asking Him to expose where your phone has become a master.

Daily Challenge

Each time you feel fear or insecurity today, quote Psalm 27:1 aloud and put your phone away.

Day 2: Search My Heart

Scripture

> *"Search me, God, and know my heart; test me and know my anxious thoughts. See if there is any offensive way in me, and lead me in the way everlasting."*
> **Psalm 139:23–24**

Lesson

Addiction thrives in denial. Freedom begins with honesty. God invites you to open your heart and let Him expose anxious thoughts and unhealthy patterns.

Reflection Questions
1. What emotions usually trigger me to reach for my phone?
2. Am I willing to let God reveal areas I've been hiding?

Action Step
Keep a journal today. Each time you feel the impulse to check your phone, record the emotion you feel.

Daily Challenge
At the end of the day, pray over your journal entries and ask God to replace each anxious thought with His peace.

Day 3: Rest in His Safety

Scripture

> *"In peace I will lie down and sleep, for you alone, Lord, make me dwell in safety."*
> **Psalm 4:8**

Lesson

Late-night scrolling robs teens of rest. God promises safety and peace when we surrender our nights to Him.

Reflection Questions

How has my phone affected my sleep?

What might I gain by ending my day in God's presence instead of online?

Action Step

Leave your phone outside your bedroom tonight. End the day in prayer and Scripture instead of scrolling.

Daily Challenge

Memorize Psalm 4:8 and recite it as your final words before sleep.

Day 4: Come to Me and Rest

Scripture

> *"Come to me, all you who are weary and burdened, and I will give you rest."*
> **Matthew 11:28**

Lesson

Social media promises escape but delivers exhaustion. Christ alone offers true rest for the soul.

Reflection Questions

Do I turn to my phone for rest more than I turn to Christ?

What burden am I carrying that I need to lay at His feet?

Action Step

Schedule a fifteen-minute break today with no phone. Use the time for prayer or quiet reflection.

Daily Challenge

Share one burden with God aloud today, then deliberately put your phone away as a sign of surrender.

Day 5: Living on God's Word
Scripture

> *"Man shall not live on bread alone, but on every word that comes from the mouth of God."*
> ***Matthew 4:4***

Lesson

Just as the body needs food, the soul needs Scripture. Social media cannot nourish your soul; it only leaves you hungrier.

Reflection Questions

How much time do I feed on digital content compared to God's Word?

Do I believe God's Word is enough to satisfy me?

Action Step

Replace fifteen minutes of scrolling with fifteen minutes of Bible reading today.

Daily Challenge

Write down one verse that speaks to you and post it somewhere you'll see it throughout the day.

Day 6: Be Still

Scripture

> *"Be still, and know that I am God."*
> **Psalm 46:10**

Lesson

Constant notifications train the mind for chaos. Stillness restores awareness of God's sovereignty.

Reflection Questions:
1. When was the last time I sat still in God's presence without distraction?
2. What keeps me from practicing stillness?

Action Step

Spend five minutes in complete silence today, without music, phone, or distractions.

Daily Challenge

Begin or end the day with five minutes of silent prayer, resisting every urge to check your phone.

Day 7: Light from the Word

Scripture:

> *"The unfolding of your words gives light; it gives understanding to the simple."*
> **Psalm 119:130**

Lesson

Social media creates confusion; God's Word gives clarity. Light from Scripture reveals truth hidden in the shadows of digital lies.

Reflection Questions
1. What lies have I believed from social media?
2. How can God's Word bring clarity into my confusion?

Action Step

Write one Bible verse on a card and carry it with you all day.

Daily Challenge

Each time you are tempted to scroll, take out the card and read the verse aloud.

Day 8: Healing Through Confession

Scripture

> *"Therefore confess your sins to each other and pray for each other so that you may be healed."*
> **James 5:16**

Lesson

Secrecy strengthens addiction; confession breaks its power. Healing begins when struggles are shared.

Reflection Questions
1. Am I willing to confess my struggles with technology to someone I trust?
2. How might prayer with others bring healing?

Action Step

Share honestly with a trusted person about your struggles with screen time.

Daily Challenge

Pray with that person and ask them to check in with you throughout the week.

Day 9: Create in Me a Pure Heart

Scripture

> *"Create in me a pure heart, O God, and renew a steadfast spirit within me."*
> **Psalm 51:10**

Lesson

Impure desires often fuel unhealthy digital habits. God alone can cleanse the heart and make it steadfast.

Reflection Questions
1. What unhealthy desires have shaped my use of social media?
2. Where do I need God to renew a steadfast spirit in me?

Action Step

Write a prayer asking God to cleanse your heart from unhealthy digital desires.

Daily Challenge

Each time you feel the pull of temptation today, pray Psalm 51:10 aloud.

Day 10: Free Indeed

Scripture

> *"So if the Son sets you free, you will be free indeed."*
> **John 8:36**

Lesson

True freedom does not come from deleting an app but from Jesus Christ. He alone breaks chains and restores life.

Reflection Questions
1. Have I trusted Christ for true freedom, or am I still relying on my own strength?
2. What victory has He already given me that I need to celebrate?

Action Step

Celebrate small victories this week by thanking God for every moment you chose Him over the scroll.

Daily Challenge

Share your testimony of one way God has helped you this week with a friend or family member.

Days 11–20: Reshaping Desires

Day 11: Hunger and Thirst for Righteousness

Scripture

> *"Blessed are those who hunger and thirst for righteousness, for they will be filled."*
> **Matthew 5:6**

Lesson

Social media whets appetites for comparison and entertainment but never truly satisfies. God promises that those who hunger for righteousness will be filled — not with fleeting dopamine but with lasting joy.

Reflection Questions
1. What am I hungering for most each day — approval online or intimacy with God?
2. Where can I redirect my cravings to be filled with His righteousness?

Action Step

Fast from social media during one meal today. Use that time to pray, read Scripture, or talk with family

Daily Challenge

Write down one area where you want God to increase your hunger for righteousness, and pray over it three times today.

Day 12: Treasures in Heaven

Scripture

> "Do not store up for yourselves treasures on earth, where moths and vermin destroy, and where thieves break in and steal. But store up for yourselves treasures in heaven."
> **Matthew 6:19–20**

Lesson

Likes and followers are fragile treasures. They can vanish overnight. Heavenly treasures — character, love, faithfulness — endure forever. Teens must choose which treasure they are pursuing.

Reflection Questions
1. How much of my energy goes tward building digital "treasures"?
2. What heavenly treasures could I pursue instead?

Action Step

Delete one app or account that fuels unhealthy comparison or temptation. Replace it with a Bible or devotional app.

Daily Challenge

Share one encouraging verse with a friend online as an act of storing up treasure in heaven.

Day 13: Seek First the Kingdom

Scripture:

> *"But seek first his kingdom and his righteousness, and all these things will be given to you as well."*
> **Matthew 6:33**

Lesson

Social media tempts teens to seek popularity first. Jesus reminds us that when God is first, everything else falls into place.

Reflection Questions
1. Do I spend my mornings seeking likes or seeking God?
2. What would my day look like if I truly sought Him first?

Action Step

Begin your day with Scripture before touching your phone.

Daily Challenge

Write Matthew 6:33 on a note and place it beside your phone as a daily reminder.

Day 14: Minds on Things Above

Scripture

> *"Set your minds on things above, not on earthly things."*
> **Colossians 3:2**

Lesson

Social media draws the mind downward, toward comparison, gossip, and envy. Scripture calls us to lift our thoughts heavenward.

Reflection Questions
1. What kind of content pulls my mind away from Christ?
2. How can I deliberately set my focus on things above?

Action Step

Post one verse, testimony, or encouragement online today as a witness.

Daily Challenge

Each time you are tempted to compare yourself today, pause and pray Colossians 3:2.

Day 15: Fruit of the Spirit

Scripture

> *"But the fruit of the Spirit is love, joy, peace, forbearance, kindness, goodness, faithfulness, gentleness and self-control."*
> **Galatians 5:22–23**

Lesson

The Spirit grows fruit that lasts. Social media feeds jealousy, anger, and pride. Teens must ask: am I producing fruit of the Spirit or fruit of the flesh?

Reflection Questions

Which fruit of the Spirit do I need most in my online life? How might self-control change the way I use social media?

Action Step

Choose one fruit of the Spirit to practice intentionally today.

Daily Challenge

At day's end, journal how you practiced that fruit instead of scrolling.

Day 16: Think About These Things

Scripture

> *"Finally, brothers and sisters, whatever is true, whatever is noble, whatever is right, whatever is pure, whatever is lovely, whatever is admirable — if anything is excellent or praiseworthy — think about such things."*
> **Philippians 4:8**

Lesson

Social media floods the mind with gossip, negativity, and impurity. God commands us to fill our thoughts with excellence and truth.

Reflection Questions

1. What thoughts dominate my mind after long scrolling sessions?
2. What practical steps can I take to think on what is pure and praiseworthy?

Action Step

Create a playlist of worship songs to replace 20 minutes of scrolling today.

Daily Challenge

Each time a negative thought arises, sing or read Philippians 4:8 aloud.

Day 17: Building Others Up

Scripture

> *"Do not let any unwholesome talk come out of your mouths, but only what is helpful for building others up according to their needs, that it may benefit those who listen."*
> **Ephesians 4:29**

Lesson

Social media often tears people down. Christ calls His followers to use their words for encouragement and life.

Reflection Questions
1. How do my online words affect others?
2. Am I building up or tearing down?

Action Step
Speak one word of encouragement in person today.

Daily Challenge
Refuse to post, share, or like anything that spreads negativity.

Day 18: A New Creation

Scripture

> *"Therefore, if anyone is in Christ, the new creation has come: The old has gone, the new is here!"*
> **2 Corinthians 5:17**

Lesson

Social media often chains teens to their past — old posts, old mistakes, old identities. Christ makes all things new.

Reflection Questions

What old identities or labels am I still holding onto? Do I believe Christ has made me new even when social media reminds me of the past?

Action Step

Write a list of the ways God has already made you new.

Daily Challenge

Destroy or delete one digital reminder of your old life that no longer reflects who you are in Christ.

Day 19: Where Your Treasure Is

Scripture

> *"For where your treasure is, there your heart will be also."*
> **Matthew 6:21**

Lesson

Our screens often reveal our true treasures. Where we invest our time, attention, and energy reveals what we love most.

Reflection Questions
1. What does my screen time reveal about my heart?
2. What would it look like if my heart treasured Christ above all else?

Action Step

Give up one full hour of social media today and use it to serve someone.

Daily Challenge

At the end of the day, journal how serving gave you greater joy than scrolling.

Day 20: God's Word as Light

Scripture

> *Your word is a lamp for my feet, a light on my path."*
> **Psalm 119:105**

Lesson
Social media can blind and confuse. God's Word provides steady light and guidance when all else fades.

Reflection Questions
1. What decisions in my life need the light of God's Word?
2. How has social media blurred my sense of direction?

Action Step
Memorize one verse this week and repeat it daily.

Daily Challenge
Each time you are tempted to scroll aimlessly, quote Psalm 119:105 and choose a purposeful action instead.

Days 21–30: Rebuilding Habits

Day 21: Do Not Give Up

Scripture

> *"Let us not become weary in doing good, for at the proper time we will reap a harvest if we do not give up."*
> **Galatians 6:9**

Lesson

Breaking free from digital addiction takes perseverance. Just as Jesus endured the cross for the joy set before Him, so must we endure the discomfort of resisting unhealthy patterns.

Reflection Questions
1. Where do I feel most weary in fighting social media addiction?
2. How can I keep my eyes on the harvest God promises?

Action Step
Commit to one daily act of service — help a parent, encourage a friend, or volunteer at church.

Daily Challenge
Each time you feel tempted to give in to scrolling, pray Galatians 6:9 and choose service instead.

Day 22: Live Wisely

Scripture

> *"Be very careful, then, how you live — not as unwise but as wise, making the most of every opportunity, because the days are evil."*
> **Ephesians 5:15–16**

Lesson

Social media steals time. God calls us to steward time wisely, making every moment count for His kingdom.

Reflection Questions

1. How much time did I waste last week scrolling?
2. What opportunities could I seize if I lived more wisely?

Action Step

Write down how much time you saved this week by reducing screen time. Choose one productive or spiritual way to use that time.

Daily Challenge

Plan one non-digital activity (like exercise, reading, or worship) for today and stick to it.

Day 23: A Living Sacrifice

Scripture

> *"Therefore, I urge you, brothers and sisters, in view of God's mercy, to offer your bodies as a living sacrifice, holy and pleasing to God — this is your true and proper worship."*
> **Romans 12:1**

Lesson

Worship is more than songs; it is surrender. Even our bodies — eyes, hands, and minds — are called to glorify God, not digital idols.

Reflection Questions:

1. Am I using my body to glorify God or to chase validation online?
2. What would it look like to offer my digital habits as worship?

Action Step

Dedicate today's physical activity (exercise, chores, or walking) as worship to God.

Daily Challenge

Each time you pick up your phone, whisper a prayer: "Lord, I give myself to You."

Day 24: God Is Close to the Brokenhearted

Scripture

> *"The Lord is close to the brokenhearted and saves those who are crushed in spirit."*
> **Psalm 34:18**

Lesson

Teens crushed by online bullying or comparison often feel abandoned. God promises His presence in the deepest pain.

Reflection Questions
1. Where has social media left me feeling brokenhearted?
2. Do I truly believe the Lord is near in those moments?

Action Step

Use freed-up time to encourage someone who is hurting.

Daily Challenge

Write Psalm 34:18 on a card and carry it with you as a reminder of God's nearness.

Day 25: The Peace of Christ

Scripture

> *"Let the peace of Christ rule in your hearts, since as members of one body you were called to peace. And be thankful."*
> **Colossians 3:15**

Lesson

Social media often stirs restlessness and discontent. Christ's peace steadies the soul and gratitude reshapes perspective.

Reflection Questions
1. What online habits disturb my peace?
2. How can gratitude restore my heart today?

Action Step

Write down five things you are thankful for instead of scrolling for entertainment.

Daily Challenge

Each time discontent arises today, recite Colossians 3:15 and thank God for His peace.

Day 26: Guard Your Company

Scripture

> *"Do not be misled: 'Bad company corrupts good character.'"*
> **1 Corinthians 15:33**

Lesson

Online influences shape character. The people we follow, watch, and admire will shape who we become.

Reflection Questions
1. Who online is influencing me most — are they leading me toward Christ or away?
2. What boundaries must I set to protect my character?

Action Step

Unfollow or mute one account that stirs envy, lust, or anger. Replace that time with reading Scripture.

Daily Challenge

Share 1 Corinthians 15:33 with a friend and talk about the importance of godly influences.

Day 27: Out of Darkness, Into Light

Scripture

> *"But you are a chosen people, a royal priesthood, a holy nation, God's special possession, that you may declare the praises of him who called you out of darkness into his wonderful light."*
> **1 Peter 2:9**

Lesson

Social media can feel like a place of darkness — gossip, bullying, and sin. God reminds His children they are chosen to live in His marvelous light.

Reflection Questions
1. Do my online habits reflect darkness or light?
2. What does it mean to me personally that I am chosen by God?

Action Step

Write a short testimony of how God has worked in your life and share it with a friend.

Daily Challenge

Post one truth or testimony about God's goodness online today.

Day 28: Build Each Other Up

Scripture

> *"Therefore encourage one another and build each other up, just as in fact you are doing."*
> **1 Thessalonians 5:11**

Lesson

While many use social media to criticize, God's people are called to encourage. True community is built through kindness and love.

Reflection Questions
1. Have my words online built people up or torn them down?
2. Who can I encourage today?

Action Step

Use social media only today to encourage or pray for others.

Daily Challenge

Choose three people online and send them a message of encouragement.

Day 29: Stand Firm in Faith

Scripture

> "Be on your guard; stand firm in the faith; be courageous; be strong. Do everything in love."
> **1 Corinthians 16:13–14**

Lesson

Social media normalizes compromise. Scripture calls believers to stand firm with courage and love.

Reflection Questions

1. Where am I most tempted to compromise my faith online?
2. How can I stand stronger in those moments?

Action Step

Set a bold boundary today — for example, no phone until after lunch.

Daily Challenge

Write 1 Corinthians 16:13–14 in your journal and pray it over yourself in the morning and evening.

Day 30: Renewed Strength

Scripture

> *"But those who hope in the Lord will renew their strength. They will soar on wings like eagles; they will run and not grow weary, they will walk and not be faint."*
> **Isaiah 40:31**

Lesson

Teens often run to social media for relief, but it leaves them weary. True renewal comes only from placing hope in the Lord.

Reflection Questions
1. What drains my strength most in digital life?
2. How has the Lord renewed me in past struggles?

Action Step

Take a phone-free walk today. As you walk, pray and reflect on God's promises of strength.

Daily Challenge

Each time you feel tired or tempted today, recite Isaiah 40:31 and claim God's renewal.

Days 31–40: Living in Freedom

Day 31: Stand Firm in Freedom

Scripture

> *"It is for freedom that Christ has set us free. Stand firm, then, and do not let yourselves be burdened again by a yoke of slavery."*
> **Galatians 5:1**

Lesson

Christ has broken the chains. The danger now is returning to old habits. Freedom must be guarded with vigilance and gratitude.

Reflection Questions
1. Where am I tempted to return to old digital habits?
2. How can I stand firm in the freedom Christ gives me?

Action Step

Reflect on your journey so far. Write down three ways God has set you free.

Daily Challenge

Share one testimony of your freedom with a trusted friend or family member.

Day 32: Armor of God

Scripture

> *"Finally, be strong in the Lord and in his mighty power. Put on the full armor of God, so that you can take your stand against the devil's schemes."*
> **Ephesians 6:10–11**

Lesson

The battle is not over. Daily we face temptation. God equips His children with spiritual armor to resist every scheme of the enemy.

Reflection Questions

1. Which piece of the armor of God do I most need to strengthen?
2. How has the enemy attacked me through social media?

Action Step

Pray through each piece of the armor of God this morning.

Daily Challenge

Write Ephesians 6:10–11 on a card and keep it visible all day as a reminder of your protection in Christ.

Day 33: Run with Perseverance

Scripture

> "Let us throw off everything that hinders and the sin that so easily entangles. And let us run with perseverance the race marked out for us, fixing our eyes on Jesus, the pioneer and perfecter of faith."
> **Hebrews 12:1–2a**

Lesson

Social media entangles like cords, but Christ calls us to throw them off. Fixing our eyes on Jesus keeps us moving forward in strength.

Reflection Questions
1. What distractions still entangle me?
2. What does it mean for me to fix my eyes on Jesus daily?

Action Step

Identify one lingering digital distraction and remove it permanently.

Daily Challenge

Each time you feel tempted today, whisper: "Jesus, my eyes are on You."

Day 34: Shine Your Light

Scripture

> *"You are the light of the world. A town built on a hill cannot be hidden."*
> **Matthew 5:14**

Lesson

Freedom is not just for personal gain but to be a testimony to others. God calls His children to shine brightly in a dark world.

Reflection Questions
1. Am I hiding my testimony of freedom?
2. Who needs to hear about God's work in my life?

Action Step

Share what God has been teaching you with a friend, small group, or youth group.

Daily Challenge

Post a Scripture or testimony online as a witness of God's light.

Day 35: Rejoice Always

Scripture

> "Rejoice always, pray continually, give thanks in all circumstances; for this is God's will for you in Christ Jesus."
> **1 Thessalonians 5:16–18**

Lesson

Gratitude shifts the heart. Social media fosters discontent, but God's will is joy, prayer, and thanksgiving.

Reflection Questions
1. Have I let social media steal my joy?
2. How can I cultivate gratitude today?

Action Step

Write down three specific blessings God gave you today and pray in thanks.

Daily Challenge

Share one word of gratitude aloud to someone today.

Day 36: Protection from the Evil One

Scripture

> *"The Lord is faithful, and he will strengthen you and protect you from the evil one."*
> **2 Thessalonians 3:3**

Lesson

Even as freedom grows, the enemy will try to pull us back. But God is faithful to protect His children.

Reflection Questions

1. Where do I most need God's protection?
2. How has He shown faithfulness in my past struggles?

Action Step

Pray a daily prayer of protection before you go online.

Daily Challenge

Each time you log in, whisper: "Lord, protect my heart and mind."

Day 37: Spur One Another On

Scripture

> *"And let us consider how we may spur one another on toward love and good deeds."*
> **Hebrews 10:24**

Lesson

Freedom is multiplied in community. Encouraging others strengthens our own resolve and builds God's kingdom.

Reflection Questions
1. Who can I encourage in their digital freedom journey?
2. How has encouragement from others helped me?

Action Step:

Encourage someone else to take a media fast and walk the journey with them.

Daily Challenge

Write an encouraging note to someone about their walk with God.

Day 38: Plans for Hope and a Future

Scripture

> *"'For I know the plans I have for you,' declares the Lord, 'plans to prosper you and not to harm you, plans to give you hope and a future.'"* J
> **Jeremiah 29:11**

Lesson

Social media often robs teens of hope by pushing unrealistic comparisons. God's Word restores vision and promise.

Reflection Questions
1. What fears about the future has social media stirred in me?
2. How does God's promise change my perspective?

Action Step
Write down three hopes or goals for life beyond social media and pray over them.

Daily Challenge
Share Jeremiah 29:11 with someone today and encourage them with God's promise.

Day 39: The Fruit of the Spirit

Scripture

> *"But the fruit of the Spirit is love, joy, peace, forbearance, kindness, goodness, faithfulness, gentleness and self-control."*
> **Galatians 5:22–23**

Lesson

Freedom bears fruit. As we walk by the Spirit, new qualities grow in our lives that cannot be manufactured by scrolling or striving.

Reflection Questions
1. Which fruit of the Spirit has grown in me most these forty days?
2. Which fruit still needs more cultivation?

Action Step

Share with someone how God has grown fruit in your life during this plan.

Daily Challenge

Practice one fruit of the Spirit intentionally today.

Day 40: To God Be the Glory

<u>Scripture</u>

> *"Now to him who is able to do immeasurably more than all we ask or imagine, according to his power that is at work within us, to him be glory in the church and in Christ Jesus throughout all generations, for ever and ever! Amen."*
> **Ephesians 3:20–21**

<u>Lesson</u>

The journey ends, but the life of freedom continues. All glory belongs to God who has done immeasurably more than we imagined.

<u>Reflection Questions</u>
1. What has God done in my life these forty days?
2. How can I continue walking in freedom after this plan?

<u>Action Step</u>
End the journey with worship. Gather family or friends, pray together, and thank God.

<u>Daily Challenge</u>
Sing a song of praise today as a declaration of victory.

Conclusion of the 40-Day Social Media Freedom Plan

This 40-day journey has not been about simply modifying behavior but transforming hearts. Through

Scripture, prayer, reflection, and practice, you have taken intentional steps to replace digital bondage with Christ-centered freedom.

If you have walked faithfully through these forty days, rejoice! You have allowed God to reshape your habits, renew your mind, and restore your communion with Him. Victory belongs to Jesus, and now you are walking in His light.

But do not stop here. Freedom is not the end — it is the beginning of a lifelong walk with God. Keep feeding your spirit daily through Bible reading, prayer, worship, and authentic community. Stay grounded in His Word, for Scripture will continue to guide you as a lamp to your feet and a light to your path (Psalm 119:105).

Lift your voice in victorious praise:

> *"Thanks be to God! He gives us the victory through our Lord Jesus Christ."*
> ***1 Corinthians 15:57***

You are free, not because of your own strength, but because the Son has set you free. And if the Son sets you free, you are free indeed (John 8:36).

So continue running the race with perseverance, fixing your eyes on Jesus, the author and perfecter of your faith. Stay rooted in His Word, for in it you will find strength, wisdom, and joy. Walk daily as a new creation, remembering: the world may offer likes, but only Christ offers life.

CHAPTER 10
RESTORING AUTHENTIC RELATIONSHIPS AND FAMILY CONNECTIONS

At the heart of social media addiction lies a tragic irony: the platforms that promise connection often deliver only isolation. God created humanity for authentic fellowship — first with Himself, and then with one another. In Genesis 2:18, God declared, "It is not good for the man to be alone. I will make a helper suitable for him." From the very beginning, human flourishing was tied to relationship. Yet many teens today are lonelier than ever, surrounded by thousands of digital "friends" yet starved for true companionship.

Authentic Relationships in a Superficial Age

Social media thrives on performance and image. Photos are filtered, captions rehearsed, and identities curated until they no longer reflect reality. Teens spend hours scrolling through highlight reels of others' lives, comparing themselves to images that are not genuine. What results is not connection but comparison, envy, and discontent.

Paul's command in Romans 12:9 speaks directly to this superficiality:

> *"Love must be sincere. Hate what is evil; cling to what is good." The Greek word Paul uses for "sincere" is anupokritos, meaning "without hypocrisy."*
> **Romans 12:9**

In other words, Christian love cannot wear a mask. Authentic relationships require honesty, vulnerability, and presence, qualities that curated digital personas cannot provide.

This principle echoes the teaching of Jesus in Matthew 23, when He rebuked the Pharisees for appearing righteous outwardly while being "full of hypocrisy and wickedness" within. Just as their outward performance masked inward emptiness, social media tempts teens to put on masks of perfection that conceal pain and loneliness. Christ's call is to live in truth, not image.

The danger of false connection is evident in research. The Pew Research Center has found that nearly half of U.S. teens report feeling lonely despite constant digital interaction. The American Psychological Association reported in 2023 that heavy social media use correlates with increased anxiety and depression, particularly among teens. Social media disciples the mind toward comparison and performance, not truth and love.

Consider a high school student named Mia. Online, her photos presented a life of popularity and perfection. Yet in private she confessed to feeling empty and unloved, desperate for someone who cared beyond the likes and comments. When a classmate finally invited her to a youth group, Mia discovered friends who prayed for her, listened without judgment, and loved sincerely. That experience taught her what Scripture had declared all along: real relationships build, not break. As 1 Thessalonians 5:11 reminds us,

> *"Therefore encourage one another and build each other up, just as in fact you are doing."*
> **1 Thessalonians 5:11**

A biblical parallel can be found in the story of Jonathan and David. In 1 Samuel 18, Jonathan's love for David was not based on performance, appearance, or popularity but on covenant loyalty. Their bond was sincere, selfless, and rooted in faith. Jonathan even risked his own future as king to defend David before his father Saul. This stands in stark contrast to superficial online "likes" that vanish when trouble arises. Teens today need relationships that resemble Jonathan's faithfulness, not fickle approval that changes with the click of a button.

The Family as God's Design for Connection

Before the church was ever established, God created the family. The command to honor father and mother in Exodus 20:12 is not simply about obedience but about nurturing the relationships that anchor identity and belonging. In the Hebrew culture, honoring parents was seen as essential to covenant blessing, for it created generational continuity of faith. Paul later affirmed this truth in Ephesians 6:2–3:

> *"Honor your father and mother — which is the first commandment with a promise — so that it may go well with you and that you may enjoy long life on the earth."*
> **Ephesians 6:2–3**

Yet today, many families have ceded this ground to screens. Teens withdraw to their bedrooms, parents scroll at the dinner table, and marriages fracture under constant distraction. Studies by Common Sense Media show that more than 70 percent of teens and nearly half of parents admit to being distracted by their phones during family time. The family altar is often replaced by the digital feed.

Scripture shows us the cost of neglecting God's design for the family. In the book of Judges, the people of Israel fell repeatedly into cycles of rebellion because "another generation grew up who knew neither the Lord nor what he had done for Israel" (Judges 2:10). Without intentional teaching in the home, faith decays. In today's world, when devices occupy more time than discipleship, the same danger looms.

But God's Word points us back to His design. Deuteronomy 6:6–7 says,

> *"These commandments that I give you today are to be on your hearts. Impress them on your children. Talk about them when you sit at home and*

> *when you walk along the road, when you lie down and when you get up."*
> **Deuteronomy 6:6–7**

The Hebrew word for "impress" implies repetition, engraving truth deeply into the heart. Families that prioritize Scripture and prayer together create roots deep enough to withstand cultural storms.

One family decided to establish "device-free dinners." At first, the silence was awkward. But soon, laughter returned, stories were shared, and prayers were spoken aloud. What began as resistance turned into joy, and the family found themselves reconnecting in ways they had long forgotten. Their practice mirrors the principle of Joshua 24:15:

> *"As for me and my household, we will serve the Lord."*
> **Joshua 24:15**

Body, Soul, and Spirit in Relationships

Authentic relationships are holistic. They do not merely touch the emotions; they nurture the whole person. The body thrives when families eat together, walk together, or play together without the interference of screens. Research shows that teens who regularly share meals with their families are less likely to engage in risky behavior and more likely to succeed academically.

The soul — the mind, will, and emotions — is nourished when genuine conversations replace superficial scrolling. Lies of comparison and envy give way to truth spoken in love. Proverbs 27:17 illustrates this:

> *"As iron sharpens iron, so one person sharpens another."*
> **Proverbs 27:17**

Social media rarely sharpens; it more often dulls through envy and distraction. But authentic fellowship brings clarity, growth, and strength.

The spirit flourishes when families pray, worship, and read Scripture together. Jesus Himself promised in Matthew 18:20,

> *"For where two or three gather in my name, there am I with them."*
> **Matthew 18:20**

When families gather in His name, even in the simplest prayers, the presence of God is near.

The Bible provides a sobering example in the household of Eli the priest. In 1 Samuel 2, Eli's sons Hophni and Phinehas despised the Lord's sacrifices and lived in unrestrained sin. Eli failed to restrain them, and judgment came upon his family. This story illustrates how neglecting the spiritual health of the family can lead to devastating consequences. In contrast, the family of Joshua was blessed because he led his household in faithful service to God.

The Church as a Restoring Community

The family is God's first community, but the church is the extended household of faith. In Acts 2:42–47, the early believers devoted themselves to teaching, fellowship, breaking bread, and prayer. Their life together was marked by authenticity, generosity, and joy. Today, the church has the opportunity to mirror this model.

The apostle Paul reminded the Galatians,

> *"Carry each other's burdens, and in this way you will fulfill the law of Christ"*
> **Galatians 6:2**

In a world of superficial online sympathy — emojis, likes, or shallow comments — the church must embody real burden-bearing. When a teen confesses struggles with online temptation, the church can provide accountability and intercession. When families feel fractured by distraction, the church can walk beside them, modeling rhythms of grace.

Biblical exegesis highlights the importance of this. The Greek word for "burden" (barē) in Galatians 6:2 suggests a heavy load that cannot be carried alone. Social media addiction and relational isolation are heavy loads for teens and families. Yet in Christ's body, no one is called to carry them alone.

Reflection

Pause for a moment and reflect: are your relationships authentic or superficial? Do your family rhythms prioritize God's design for fellowship, or have they been displaced by constant scrolling? Begin small. Reclaim one meal each day as sacred. Read Scripture aloud, pray together, and allow honest conversation to take place.

Authentic relationships and restored family connections are not optional luxuries — they are lifelines. Jesus said in John 13:35,

> *"By this everyone will know that you are my disciples, if you love one another."*
> **John 13:35**

In a digital world obsessed with curated images and shallow likes, it is sincere, Christlike love that marks the people of God. Families who commit to love one another deeply, and churches that foster this commitment, stand as beacons of light in a world desperate for authenticity.

CHAPTER 11
REBUILDING BIBLICAL COMMUNITY IN A DIGITAL WORLD

God never intended His people to live in isolation. From the very beginning, He said,

> *"It is not good for the man to be alone."*
> **Genesis 2:18**

Community was not an afterthought but part of God's design for human flourishing. Humanity was created for fellowship with God and with one another. Throughout Scripture, His plan has always been communal—Israel as a chosen nation, the early church as a Spirit-filled family of believers, and the body of Christ as a living, interconnected organism.

Yet social media, though it claims to connect, has instead contributed to loneliness and shallow relationships. Studies by the American Psychological Association show that teens who spend more than three hours a day online are significantly more likely to report feelings of isolation and sadness. Another nationwide survey from Cigna reported that over 60% of young people describe themselves as "lonely," despite being digitally "connected" to hundreds or even thousands of online contacts. Social media creates an illusion of fellowship, but without the substance of real connection, it often leaves the soul starved for authentic community.

The Nature of True Community

True biblical community is not based on likes, comments, or curated images. It is rooted in Christ and characterized by love, truth, vulnerability, and mutual care. The early church demonstrated this powerfully. Luke records:

> *"They devoted themselves to the apostles' teaching and to fellowship, to the breaking of bread and to prayer. Everyone was filled with awe at the many wonders and signs performed by the apostles. All the believers were together and had everything in common."*
> ***Acts 2:42–44***

This was not shallow interaction but a radical sharing of life. They ate together, prayed together, confessed their sins together, and carried each other's burdens. Compare this to the digital culture where attention is fragmented, conversations are brief, and relationships are measured by algorithms. Authentic fellowship is not found in a comment thread; it is born in eye contact, shared meals, and time spent walking side by side.

For teens, this means moving beyond the curated image they maintain online. A young girl named Emily once confessed, "I have hundreds of friends online but no one I can really talk to." Her story is not rare. In truth, she was surrounded by digital connection but deprived of true friendship. It was not until she joined a small group at her church, where she could be known, prayed for, and cared for, that she began to taste the joy of biblical community.

The Call to Fellowship

The book of Hebrews exhorts:

> *"And let us consider how we may spur one another on toward love and good deeds, not giving up meeting together, as some are in the habit of doing, but encouraging one another — and all the more as you see the Day approaching."*
> ***(Hebrews 10:24–25)***

The command to gather is not optional; it is essential for spiritual survival.

The digital world makes gathering seem unnecessary. Why go to church when you can watch a livestream? Why meet a friend when you can text? Why confess your struggles when you can post a filtered update that hides the truth? But the early Christians risked their lives to meet together in homes and catacombs. They understood what many teens today are missing: that true fellowship cannot be digitized. It requires presence. It requires sacrifice. It requires love.

Biblical community calls us to move beyond convenience. A message of encouragement on Snapchat cannot compare to kneeling in prayer beside a struggling friend. A "like" on an Instagram post does not heal the soul the way the touch of a hand or the presence of a caring mentor does.

Community as a Safeguard Against Sin

Isolation is dangerous because it leaves us vulnerable. Ecclesiastes 4:9–10 declares:

> *"Two are better than one, because they have a good return for their labor: If either of them falls down, one can help the other up. But pity anyone who falls and has no one to help them up."*
> ***Ecclesiastes 4:9–10***

The truth is sobering: teens who isolate themselves are far more likely to fall into depression, risky behaviors, and even suicide. A 2023 CDC report revealed that 30% of teen girls seriously considered suicide in the past year, a number worsened by cyberbullying and digital isolation.

James reminds us of the protective power of community:

> *"Therefore confess your sins to each other and pray for each other so that you may be healed."*
> ***James 5:16***

Healing flows in the context of honesty before others. Satan thrives in secrecy, whispering that struggles must be hidden. But biblical fellowship pulls back the curtain, breaks the lies, and offers accountability that leads to freedom.

Scripture offers us sobering examples of what happens when isolation takes root. King David, when he distanced himself from his responsibilities and withdrew into idleness, fell into sin with Bathsheba (2 Samuel 11). Cut off from accountability, his soul faltered. Contrast this with the strength of Paul, who traveled with companions like Timothy, Barnabas, and Silas. His ministry thrived because he was never truly alone.

Body, Soul, and Spirit in Community

Biblical community restores balance to the whole person. The body experiences renewal when rhythms of worship, meals, and recreation are shared. Families who eat together regularly show lower rates of teen depression and substance abuse, according to a study published by the National Center on Addiction and Substance Abuse. The soul is nurtured when lies are replaced with encouragement, when real conversations take the place of superficial scrolling. And the spirit is strengthened when prayer and worship are shared among believers, for Jesus promised,

> *"Where two or three gather in my name, there am I with them."*
> **Matthew 18:20**

A teenage boy named Marcus once described how lonely he felt even while gaming online for hours with "friends." But when he joined a local youth Bible study, he said, "It felt like I finally had brothers. They prayed for me. They knew my name. They noticed when I was missing." His story echoes the reality that online friendships may entertain but cannot replace the deep nourishment of Christ-centered fellowship.

Practical Paths to Rebuild Biblical Community

Rebuilding biblical community requires intentionality. It may look like small groups where teens and adults meet weekly to study Scripture and share struggles. It may be families who commit to digital fasts during meals and set aside nights for games and devotion. It may even be church-wide retreats that strip away phones for a weekend of prayer, worship, and real human presence.

One church hosted a "Digital Detox Weekend." Teens left their phones at the door and spent forty-eight hours in worship, service projects, and time outdoors. At first, many were restless and anxious. But by Sunday, testimonies poured out: "I never realized how much peace I was missing," one said. Another admitted, "I actually heard God's voice again."

The path is not about rejecting technology completely but reclaiming what it has stolen: true fellowship, grounded in love, strengthened by prayer, and rooted in Christ.

Chapter 11 Reflection

Ask yourself: do your friendships reflect the pattern of this world or the pattern of Christ? Are your connections shallow and fleeting, or do they reflect the love that

> *"always protects, always trusts, always hopes, always perseveres"*
> **1 Corinthians 13:7?**

This week, take a step toward deeper community. Join a small group, invite a friend to pray with you, or commit to one device-free meal with your family. In doing so, you will not only resist the insidious pull of social media but also rediscover the joy of God's design for community.

Biblical fellowship is not an accessory to faith; it is its lifeblood. As Jesus declared:

> *"By this everyone will know that you are my disciples, if you love one another."*
> **(John 13:35).**

In a digital world desperate for real love, may your life and your relationships bear witness to the love of Christ.

CHAPTER 12
THE ROLE OF THE CHURCH IN A DIGITAL WORLD

The fight against social media addiction is not an individual battle alone; it is a communal one. God never intended His people to struggle in isolation. The Church is the body of Christ, called to bear one another's burdens and to stand together against the enemy. Paul reminds us:

> *"Now you are the body of Christ, and each one of you is a part of it."*
> **1 Corinthians 12:27**

Every member matters, and every member has a role to play in the healing, restoration, and discipleship of the next generation.

The Church as a Place of Healing

The Church must be a safe place where teens and parents can confess struggles without fear of condemnation. Galatians 6:2 instructs:

> *"Carry each other's burdens, and in this way you will fulfill the law of Christ."*
> **Galatians 6:2**

Healing begins when the Church creates space for honesty, grace, and restoration. Addiction thrives in secrecy, but the presence of Christ among His people offers a place for freedom.

A modern example can be seen in a church that began hosting "Family Media Fasts," where once a month, families committed to spending a weekend without screens. They gathered for worship, meals, and service projects. The result was not just reduced screen time but deeper connection, stronger faith, and renewed joy. In these moments of shared struggle and healing, the Church lived out its calling as a place of hope.

The Church as a Place of Discipleship

The Church must also be a place of intentional teaching, where Scripture is lifted above culture and truth is proclaimed clearly. Jesus promised,

> *"Then you will know the truth, and the truth will set you free."*
> **John 8:32**

Pastors and leaders cannot afford to ignore the influence of social media on teens. They must equip believers with biblical wisdom to navigate the digital age.

One church developed a discipleship program for teens called "Truth Over Trends," combining Bible study with media literacy. Teens compared what Scripture said about identity, purity, and contentment with the messages they encountered online. Over time, they testified that the program helped them resist temptation and live more Christ-centered lives. Discipleship in today's church must be bold, relevant, and deeply rooted in God's Word.

The Church as a Place of Community

Isolation fuels addiction, but community breaks its power. Hebrews 10:24–25 exhorts:

> *"And let us consider how we may spur one another on toward love and good deeds, not giving up meeting together, as some are in the habit of doing, but encouraging one another — and all the more as you see the Day approaching."*
> **Hebrews 10:24–25**

Youth groups, family gatherings, and intergenerational relationships provide the encouragement teens need to persevere. One church youth group created a "Digital Detox Retreat," where teens surrendered their phones for a weekend and instead spent time in worship, games, testimonies, and prayer. By the end of the retreat, many shared that they had never felt more connected, not only to each other but also to God.

Community is not optional. It is God's antidote to isolation, and the Church must reclaim its place as a family where no one walks alone.

The Early Church as Our Model

Luke describes the life of the first believers in Acts 2:42–47:

> *"They devoted themselves to the apostles' teaching and to fellowship, to the breaking of bread and to prayer. Everyone was filled with awe at the many wonders and signs performed by the apostles. All the believers were together and had everything in common. They sold property and possessions to give to anyone who had need. Every day they continued to meet together in the temple courts. They broke bread in their homes and ate together with glad and sincere hearts, praising God and enjoying the favor of all the people. And the Lord added to their number daily those who were being saved."*
> ***Acts 2:42–47***

This description of the early church provides a blueprint for today's Church to respond to the spiritual dangers of social media. Each characteristic of Acts 2 reveals what is missing in much of modern culture and how the Church can step in to fill the void.

Devotion to the Apostles' Teaching

The early believers grounded their lives in truth, while today's teens are discipled by influencers and algorithms. A teen named Jason struggled with feelings of worthlessness amplified by Instagram. Through a Bible study on Ephesians led by his youth pastor, Jason came to understand that in Christ he was chosen, adopted, and dearly loved. This shift in his thinking broke the hold of comparison. The Church today must be bold in teaching Scripture as the antidote to digital lies.

Fellowship

True fellowship goes deeper than likes or follows. Emily, a teen who felt invisible in her church, found authentic belonging when she joined a small group that met weekly for prayer and encouragement. Over time, she realized that the friendships she built in Christ were stronger than the superficial connections she pursued online. Just as the early church devoted themselves to fellowship, the Church today must help teens rediscover what it means to be truly known.

Breaking of Bread

The early church shared meals, creating space for honesty and gratitude. In contrast, screens now dominate family tables. One family instituted "screen-free dinners," and slowly discovered that conversations, laughter, and prayers filled the space once occupied by silence and distraction. During one dinner, their son shared that he was being bullied online — a struggle that would have remained hidden without this intentional time together. The Church can encourage these rhythms, restoring the sacredness of shared meals.

Prayer

Prayer was central to the early church and must be central today. Marcus, a teen trapped in pornography he discovered through social media, found freedom when his small group surrounded him in prayer. They prayed with him, encouraged him, and reminded him of God's promises. Over time, Marcus saw progress he could never have achieved alone. The Church today must be a praying people, because prayer is the weapon that breaks digital chains.

Generosity

The early church gave sacrificially to meet one another's needs. Social media fuels greed and envy, but generosity flips the script. Sophia, a teen constantly pressured by online fashion trends, joined her youth group in donating clothes to a shelter. Giving away her favorite shoes, she discovered joy in generosity that no online purchase had ever brought her. Generosity transforms hearts, and the Church must model it in an age of consumerism.

Worship

Acts describes believers praising God together. Worship shifts focus away from screens and onto Christ. Liam, a teen who drowned his anxiety in TikTok, found peace during a youth worship night when he encountered God's presence. Worship helped him replace distraction with devotion. Like the early church, today's Church must be a worshiping community, lifting eyes and hearts above the digital noise.

Daily Togetherness

The early church met daily in homes and in the temple courts. Their faith was not confined to one day a week. In a culture where teens spend hours isolated in bedrooms with their devices, daily togetherness is revolutionary. A group of students began gathering before school for morning prayer. What began as a discipline became their favorite part of the day, drawing them closer to God and to each other. This rhythm mirrors the early believers and reminds us that discipleship is a daily practice.

Body, Soul, and Spirit in Community

Biblical community restores the whole person. The body is renewed through rhythms of rest, meals, and service. The soul is strengthened by encouragement, confession, and accountability. The spirit is nourished through corporate prayer, worship, and the presence of the Holy Spirit. Social media offers only an illusion of connection, but the Church offers life.

Jesus said,

> *"By this everyone will know that you are my disciples, if you love one another."*
> ***John 13:35***

Love expressed in authentic community is the answer to loneliness and the cure for addiction's isolation.

Chapter 12 Reflection

What does true community look like in your life? Are your friendships shallow or deep? Do you have brothers and sisters who walk with you, pray with you, and encourage you? Take one step this week to move from digital connection to biblical community: join a small group, invite a friend to dinner, or spend time with others in prayer and fellowship.

The Church is not perfect, but it is God's chosen instrument for discipleship, healing, and community. By following the pattern of Acts 2 and reclaiming authentic fellowship, the Church today can break the grip of social media's counterfeit connections and lead a generation into true freedom in Christ.

CHAPTER 13
A GENERATION REDEEMED – FINAL CHARGE

The story of this book has been sobering. We have seen how social media, though not evil in itself, has become an insidious snare, luring countless teens into addiction, robbing families of connection, and leading souls into darkness. We have also seen the greater truth: in Christ, there is hope, freedom, and redemption. The battle is fierce, but the victory belongs to the Lord.

The Call to a Redeemed Generation

Scripture paints a vision of what a redeemed generation looks like. Peter wrote: "But you are a chosen people, a royal priesthood, a holy nation, God's special possession, that you may declare the praises of him who called you out of darkness into his wonderful light." (1 Peter 2:9). Teens and families are not destined to be slaves to algorithms, trends, or temptations. They are called to be a holy generation, set apart for God's glory.

To be a chosen generation means that God has handpicked you for this time in history. He has not left you at the mercy of culture, but has equipped you with His Spirit to stand firm. To be a royal priesthood means that you represent God's presence on earth — your words, your actions, your witness matter. The priesthood in Israel stood between God and the people, offering sacrifices and prayers. Today, teens who follow Christ stand as intercessors for their peers, carrying the message of hope into places darkened by digital idolatry.

Paul exhorts the young believer Timothy:

> *"Don't let anyone look down on you because you are young, but set an example for the believers in speech, in conduct, in love, in faith and in purity."*
> ***1 Timothy 4:12***

This is the call for today's teens: not to follow the crowd, not to conform to the world, but to lead by example in holiness, courage, and love.

From Darkness to Light

Jesus declared:

> *"You are the light of the world. A town built on a hill cannot be hidden. Neither do people light a lamp and put it under a bowl. Instead they put it on its stand, and it gives light to everyone in the house. In the same way, let your light shine before*

> *others, that they may see your good deeds and glorify your Father in heaven."*
> **Matthew 5:14–16**

A redeemed generation shines as light in the darkness. While peers are consumed with comparison and performance, redeemed teens point to Christ as the source of identity and worth. While others hide behind screens, redeemed families gather around God's Word. While culture normalizes rebellion, redeemed communities honor authority and pursue holiness.

The apostle Paul reminds us of the daily choice before every believer:

> *"For you were once darkness, but now you are light in the Lord. Live as children of light."*
> **Ephesians 5:8**

Walking in the light means honesty, purity, and faithfulness. Social media may magnify darkness — comparison, lust, anger, and pride — but Christ calls His people to walk openly in the truth.

The Role of Parents and Leaders

Parents and church leaders play a vital role in this redemption story. Moses commanded Israel:

> *"These commandments that I give you today are to be on your hearts. Impress them on your children. Talk about them when you sit at home and when you walk along the road, when you lie down and when you get up."*
> **Deuteronomy 6:6–7**

The spiritual formation of the next generation is not the responsibility of schools or screens; it is the sacred calling of families and the church.

When parents model restraint, love, and devotion to God, children learn to do the same. When pastors and youth leaders teach the dangers of sin and the hope of Christ with clarity and compassion, young hearts are anchored in truth. A redeemed generation will rise when older generations are faithful in their calling.

Scripture also reminds us of the partnership between generations:

> *"The glory of young men is their strength, gray hair the splendor of the old."*
> **Proverbs 20:29**

The old bring wisdom and experience, the young bring energy and strength. Together, families and churches can unite across generations to resist the schemes of the enemy. With the wisdom of mentors and the strength of young believers, the body of Christ is fully equipped to raise up a redeemed generation.

Body, Soul, and Spirit of a Redeemed Generation

The work of redemption transforms the whole person. The body is disciplined, using strength and energy not for self-indulgence but for service. The soul is renewed, governed by the Spirit, with thoughts, emotions, and desires aligned to God's Word. The spirit is alive, empowered by the Holy Spirit to resist temptation, proclaim the gospel, and walk in holiness.

Paul's prayer captures this vision:

> *"May God himself, the God of peace, sanctify you through and through. May your whole spirit, soul and body be kept blameless at the coming of our Lord Jesus Christ. The one who calls you is faithful, and he will do it."*
> ***1 Thessalonians 5:23–24***

A redeemed generation is one that experiences this sanctification in every part of life.

A Final Charge

The battle for this generation's souls is real, but so is the victory of Christ. Teens, you do not have to be slaves to your screens. Parents, you are not powerless in this fight. Leaders, you are not laboring in vain. The power of the gospel is sufficient to redeem, restore, and renew.

Joshua's words echo across the centuries:

> *"But if serving the Lord seems undesirable to you, then choose for yourselves this day whom you will serve... But as for me and my household, we will serve the Lord."*
> ***Joshua 24:15***

The choice is before us: conformity to the world, or transformation by Christ. Addiction to the scroll, or freedom in the Spirit. Darkness, or light.

This is the call to walk in the Spirit. Paul writes:

> *"So I say, walk by the Spirit, and you will not gratify the desires of the flesh."*
> **Galatians 5:16**

Again, he declares:

> *"For those who are led by the Spirit of God are the children of God."*
> **Romans 8:14**

Teens must see that the soul is the battleground — between the flesh, which is subject to the ruler of this world, and the Spirit, who leads us into truth. To walk with Christ is to declare victory over every temptation and to claim the freedom already won on the cross.

Satan comes only to kill, steal, and destroy. Jesus says:

> *"I have come that they may have life, and have it to the full."*
> **John 10:10**

This is the promise of a redeemed generation. The devil's schemes are strong, but they cannot overcome the Spirit of God. James assures us:

> *"Resist the devil, and he will flee from you."*
> **James 4:7**

This resistance is not passive but active, daily choosing Christ over compromise, light over darkness, truth over lies.

Chapter 13 Reflection

Ask yourself: What will define my generation? Will it be distraction, despair, and digital slavery? Or will it be redemption, restoration, and revival? The answer is not in technology but in Christ.

Pray this prayer aloud: "Lord Jesus, we choose You. Redeem our generation. Free us from the snares of addiction. Restore our families. Revive our churches. Let us be a generation marked not by screens, but by Your Spirit. Amen."

This is not the end, but the beginning. A redeemed generation will shine light in the darkest places, bear the strength of youth and the wisdom of elders, and proclaim Christ to a world enslaved by false idols. Teens, you are chosen. You are a royal priesthood. You are set apart for God's glory. Rise up, walk in the Spirit, and let the world see the radiance of Christ in you.

CONCLUSION
WALKING IN THE LIGHT

This book began with a sobering story of loss. It traced the dangers of social media addiction and the spiritual warfare behind it. But it ends with hope. The same Christ who overcame the wilderness, who triumphed over the grave, and who poured out His Spirit on His people is the Christ who calls this generation out of darkness and into light.

> *"For you were once darkness, but now you are light in the Lord. Live as children of light."*
> **Ephesians 5:8**

Freedom is possible. Authentic relationships can be restored. Families can be healed. Churches can be rebuilt. A generation can be redeemed. The glow of a screen is no match for the glory of the risen Christ.

So take courage. Walk in the light. And remember: the battle for a generation's souls is not fought alone. It is fought in the strength of the Lord, by the truth of

His Word, and in the fellowship of His people. Victory is certain, because the Light has already come, and the darkness cannot overcome it (John 1:5).

From Darkness to Light

We have seen how what begins as curiosity on a glowing screen can lead into the depths of despair. The cries of teens like Hannah remind us that cruel words online can crush the soul. Studies confirm what Scripture already revealed: isolation, comparison, and ridicule lead to anxiety, depression, and even suicide. Yet we were never meant to live in darkness. From the beginning God separated light from darkness, calling His people to walk in truth, holiness, and love.

The Nature of Sin and the Power of Grace

We uncovered how the seven deadly sins thrive in the digital age. Pride parades itself in followers, envy festers in comparison, wrath strikes in comments, sloth numbs through endless scrolling, greed consumes in ads, lust lures in images, and gluttony thrives in endless consumption. And Scripture reminds us,

> *"The wages of sin is death, but the gift of God is eternal life in Christ Jesus our Lord."*
> **Romans 6:23**

For every chain of sin, Christ offers freedom. Where pride destroys, humility in Christ restores. Where lust enslaves, purity in Christ redeems. Where wrath poisons, gentleness in Christ brings peace.

The Law of God and the Call of Christ

We remembered the Ten Commandments — not as relics, but as living truth. God gave them to protect His people, to guard their souls, and to anchor them in His holiness. And Christ summed them into two great commandments: to love the Lord with all our heart, soul, and mind, and to love our neighbor as ourselves. Social media cannot teach this love, for its pattern is often selfishness, competition, and performance. Yet love covers a multitude of sins, and in love we find freedom.

The War for the Soul

We looked at the reality of addiction. Medical science tells us that dopamine surges fuel compulsion, while statistics reveal that most teens spend nearly seven hours a day online. But Scripture tells us this is more than a neurological issue — it is spiritual warfare.

> *"For our struggle is not against flesh and blood, but against the rulers, against the authorities, against the powers of this dark world and against the spiritual forces of evil in the heavenly realms."*
> **Ephesians 6:12**

Yet God has given His people armor, and with the belt of truth, the shield of faith, and the sword of the Spirit, we are more than conquerors.

Boundaries, Renewal, and Reset

We learned that boundaries are not chains but safeguards, and that renewal is not optional but essential. Teens who set aside their phones at night gain rest for their bodies. Families who choose device-free dinners find fellowship restored. Churches that teach renewal of the mind discover lives transformed. Scripture says,

> *"Do not conform to the pattern of this world, but be transformed by the renewing of your mind."*
> **Romans 12:2**

Renewal is not just a mental shift; it is a spiritual reorientation where Christ becomes the center again.

The Freedom of Confession and Accountability

We saw how confession breaks chains. Addiction thrives in secrecy, but healing begins in the light.

> *"If we confess our sins, he is faithful and just and will forgive us our sins and purify us from all unrighteousness."*
> **1 John 1:9**

And accountability sustains the journey, as

> *"a cord of three strands is not quickly broken."*
> **Ecclesiastes 4:12**

Teens who find trusted mentors, parents who confess struggles honestly, churches that open space for grace — these become communities of freedom.

The Practice of Renewal Through the Word

We were reminded that the battlefield is the mind.

> *"As a man thinks in his heart, so is he."*
> **Proverbs 23:7**

To think on what is true, noble, right, pure, lovely, admirable, excellent, and praiseworthy is to let God's Word shape the soul. Every notification may whisper lies, but the Word speaks truth. Teens who fill their minds with Scripture rather than scrolling will find themselves walking in the Spirit, not gratifying the desires of the flesh.

A Journey of Freedom

We walked through a forty-day plan of freedom — a spiritual detox from the toxins of social media. Just as God caused the rain to fall for forty days to cleanse the earth in Genesis, and just as Christ fasted forty days to prepare for His mission, so too can teens and families embrace a season of discipline and renewal. Freedom is possible because Christ sets us free, and

> *"if the Son sets you free, you will be free indeed."*
> **John 8:36**

Restoring Relationships and Community

We rediscovered the power of authentic relationships and the irreplaceable role of family. Screens cannot replace shared meals, honest conversations, and heartfelt prayers. And we saw that the Church —

the body of Christ — must rise again as the place of healing, discipleship, and fellowship. Just as the early believers devoted themselves to teaching, prayer, and breaking bread, so must we reclaim the rhythms of biblical community.

A Final Charge for a Redeemed Generation

We conclude with the call of redemption. Teens, you are a chosen generation and a royal priesthood. Parents, you are entrusted with the sacred call of discipleship. Leaders, you are called to shepherd faithfully. The old bring wisdom; the young bring strength. Together, in Christ, a generation can rise.

Joshua's words remain a charge:

> *"But as for me and my household, we will serve the Lord."*
> **Joshua 24:15**

The choice is before us still — to conform to the world or to be transformed by Christ. To live in darkness or to shine as light.

A Benediction of Hope

And so, we end not in despair but in victory. May this generation walk in the light as He is in the light. May the body, soul, and spirit of every teen be sanctified wholl by the God of peace. May families be restored, churches revived, and communities renewed.

> **"The Lord bless you and keep you; the Lord make his face shine on you and be gracious**

> ***to you; the Lord turn his face toward you and give you peace." (Numbers 6:24–26).***

Take courage, beloved of God. The battle for a generation's souls is real, but the victory is already won. Christ is the Light, and the darkness cannot overcome Him.

AFTERWORD
CHOOSING GOD OVER THE SCROLL

The book may have ended, but your journey has not. Freedom in Christ is not a moment — it is a daily walk. Every day you face a choice: will you fill your soul with the noise of the world, or with the voice of God?

Jesus said,

> *"But seek first his kingdom and his righteousness, and all these things will be given to you as well."*
> **Matthew 6:33**

Social media urges you to seek approval, likes, and recognition. But God invites you to seek Him first. He promises that in His presence you will find strength, peace, and purpose. Paul wrote,

> *"Set your minds on things above, not on earthly things."*
> **Colossians 3:2**

Each notification is an invitation to distraction, but each moment with God is an invitation to transformation. The soul will always be hungry — the question is what you will feed it.

So begin small. Before opening your phone in the morning, open your Bible. Before checking notifications at night, lift your heart in prayer. Every time you feel the urge to scroll, ask instead: What if I spent these minutes with God? Over time, those small choices become a lifestyle of freedom.

Remember the words of Jesus:

> *"Come to me, all you who are weary and burdened, and I will give you rest."*
> **Matthew 11:28**

Social media cannot give you rest. Only Christ can. He is the Friend who never unfollows, the Shepherd who never abandons, the Light who never dims.

Choose Him daily. Let His Word be the feed you scroll, His presence the message you wait for, His Spirit the One who shapes your identity. And as you do, you will discover that the joy of walking with God far outweighs the fleeting pull of any screen.

> *"Delight yourself in the Lord, and he will give you the desires of your heart."*
> **Psalm 37:4**

REFERENCES CITED

American Academy of Pediatrics. (2016). Media and Young Minds. Pediatrics, 138(5).

American Psychological Association. (2019). Social media and teen mental health.

American Psychological Association. (2023). Health advisory on social media use in adolescence. Washington, DC.

American Psychological Association. (2023). Social Media and Youth Mental Health: Current Trends. Retrieved from https://www.apa.org

Barna Group. (2022). The open generation: How teens around the world relate to Jesus.

Centers for Disease Control and Prevention. (2023). Youth Risk Behavior Survey Data Summary & Trends Report. Retrieved from https://www.cdc.gov

Cigna. (2021). Loneliness in America: How the pandemic has deepened an epidemic of loneliness and what we can do about it.

Common Sense Media. (2022). The Common Sense census: Media use by tweens and teens. San Francisco, CA.

Education Week. New Data Reveal How Many Students Are Using AI to Cheat (teacher survey, 2023–24). (Education Week)

Gallup. (2023). Teens average 4.8 hours per day on social media. Gallup Polling Report.

Lembke, A. (2021). Dopamine Nation: Finding Balance in the Age of Indulgence. New York: Dutton.

Lifeway Research. (2019). Discipleship and small group participation survey.

Meyer, J. (2002). Battlefield of the Mind. FaithWords.

National Center on Addiction and Substance Abuse. (2012). The importance of family dinners VIII.

National Center for Missing & Exploited Children (NCMEC). CyberTipline Reports: 2023 Annual Data and 2024/2025 updates on online enticement and CSAM files. (NCMEC, Thorn)

National Institute on Drug Abuse. (2023). Adolescent brain development and vulnerability to addiction. Bethesda, MD.

National Institute on Drug Abuse. (2023). Monitoring the Future survey results. Bethesda, MD.

National Institute of Mental Health. (2022). Technology and Youth Mental Health. Retrieved from https://www.nimh.nih.gov

Office of Juvenile Justice and Delinquency Prevention. (2022). Juvenile Justice Statistics. Washington, DC.

Office of Juvenile Justice and Delinquency Prevention. (2022). Youth and the Juvenile Justice System: 2022 National Report. Washington, DC: U.S. Department of Justice.

OJJDP Model Programs Guide. Bullying and Cyberbullying: Literature Review (updated 2023). (purl.fdlp.gov)

Pew Research Center. (2022). Teens, Social Media and Technology 2022. Retrieved from https://www.pewresearch.org

Sabina, C., Wolak, J., & Finkelhor, D. (2008). The nature and dynamics of Internet pornography exposure for youth. CyberPsychology & Behavior, 11(6), 691–693.

Temple, J. R., Choi, H. J., Reuter, T., & Wolfe, D. A. (2013). Impact of exposure to sexual violence in adolescence. Journal of Adolescent Health, 53(6), 757–763.

The Trevor Project. (2022). National Survey on LGBTQ Youth Mental Health 2022. New York, NY.

U.S. Department of Justice. (2022). Youth and Social Media: Impacts on Crime and Delinquency. Office of Justice Programs.

SMALL GROUP RESOURCES

Foreword to Study Resources

These study tools are designed to help teens, parents, and church leaders engage with the truths of Insidious Social Media: The Battle for a Generation's Souls in a practical, interactive way.

The Teen Small Group Participant Guide provides a 8-week journey through the book. The guide gives chapter-by-chapter summaries, Scriptures, discussion questions, and personal applications. The Small Group Leader's Guide equips leaders to facilitate meaningful sessions, offering teaching notes, discussion flow, and prayer prompts. For additional leader's support be sure to read the Small Group Leader's Support Training at the end of The Small Group Leader's Guide.

Whether used in youth groups, family discipleship, or church small groups, these resources are intended to strengthen accountability, deepen understanding, and point every reader back to the freedom that comes through Christ alone.

Teen Small Group Participant Guide

How to Use This Guide

This guide is designed to walk with you over eight weeks as you confront social media addiction and discover freedom in Christ. Each week will guide you through reading from the book, a summary of its key truths, Scripture to meditate on, three discussion questions for group study, a life application to put the lesson into practice, and an action item to help you take one concrete step toward freedom.

You will also complete a Digital Addiction Assessment in Week 2. This will help you see where your habits may be shaping your life and will guide deeper reflection during the weeks that follow. Be honest — your healing begins with truth.

Bring this guide with you each week, read the passages, reflect on the questions, and pray that God would open your heart. Remember, you are not alone in this battle. You belong to Christ, you belong to His Church, and you belong to a generation that can be redeemed.

Week 1 – Light vs. Darkness

Reading Plan: Introduction and Chapter 1.

Summary
Social media presents itself as light, but behind the screen hides darkness. Comparison corrodes joy, envy poisons gratitude, lust defiles purity, wrath wounds with words, and despair steals life. Christ alone is the true Light. Walking with Him means stepping out of darkness and living in His truth.

Key Scripture

> *"This is the message we have heard from him and declare to you: God is light; in him there is no darkness at all. If we claim to have fellowship with him and yet walk in the darkness, we lie and do not live out the truth. But if we walk in the light, as he is in the light, we have fellowship with one another, and the blood of Jesus, his Son, purifies us from all sin."*
> **1 John 1:5–7**

Discussion Questions

1. In what ways does social media act like "false light"?
2. How do you see teens around you struggling with darkness behind their screens?
3. What would it look like for you to walk in the Light of Christ this week?

Life Application

Start every morning this week by reading one psalm before checking your phone. Notice the difference in how your day begins.

Action Item

Share Psalm 119:105 with a friend or family member: "Your word is a lamp for my feet, a light on my path."

Week 2 – Facing the Battle Within
(Addiction Assessment)

Reading Plan: Chapter 2 and the Addiction Assessment in Chapter 6.

Summary

The seven deadly sins — pride, envy, wrath, sloth, greed, lust, and gluttony — are magnified through social media. They enslave the soul, weaken the body, and darken the spirit. This week you will also complete a Digital Addiction Assessment to measure how deeply social media affects your life. This is not about shame; it is about truth that sets free.

Key Scripture

> *"So if the Son sets you free, you will be free indeed."*
> **John 8:36**

Discussion Questions

1. Which deadly sin do you see most on social media?
2. What did you learn from your addiction assessment about your own habits?
3. How does Christ offer freedom in the areas where you struggle most?

Life Application

Confess one area of struggle to God this week and ask Him for strength.

Action Item
Share John 8:36 with your group and declare aloud that freedom is possible in Christ.

Week 3 – God's Commandments and the Soul

Reading Plan: Chapter 3.

Summary

God gave the Ten Commandments as life-giving boundaries, not burdens. Teens often break them online through idolatry, dishonor, lust, theft, lies, and coveting. Christ calls us back to holiness and truth. Each commandment protects relationships with God and with others.

Key Scripture

> *"You shall have no other gods before me."*
> **Exodus 20:3**

Discussion Questions

1. How can social media become an idol in your life?
2. Which commandment do you most struggle to keep in the digital world?
3. How can obedience protect you from harm?

Life Application

Take a one-day fast from one digital habit this week (such as TikTok, Snapchat, or gaming). Notice how it changes your thoughts and feelings.

Action Item: Post or share one of the Ten Commandments with a positive message for friends.

Week 4 – Addiction and Spiritual Warfare

Reading Plan: Chapter 4.

Summary

Social media addiction rewires the brain through dopamine release and creates footholds for the enemy. Behind every sinful action is a deeper spiritual war. But God has given us His armor to stand firm: truth, righteousness, faith, salvation, peace, and the Word.

Key Scripture:

> *"For our struggle is not against flesh and blood, but against the rulers, against the authorities, against the powers of this dark world and against the spiritual forces of evil in the heavenly realms."*
> **Ephesians 6:12**

Discussion Questions
1. What habits of yours feel more like bondage than freedom?
2. Why is it important to see addiction as spiritual warfare and not just bad habits?
3. Which piece of God's armor do you need most right now?

Life Application

Memorize one verse from Ephesians 6 about the armor of God this week.

Action Item

Replace one hour of scrolling with one hour of prayer, journaling, or listening to worship music.

Week 5 – Boundaries and Spiritual Reset

Reading Plan: Chapter 5.

Summary

Freedom from social media addiction requires both wise boundaries and a spiritual reset. Boundaries guard against bondage, while reset restores what is broken. Teens must set limits on time, friendships, and activities, while reorienting their minds and hearts to Christ.

Key Scripture

> "'I have the right to do anything,' you say — but not everything is beneficial. 'I have the right to do anything' — but I will not be mastered by anything."
> **1 Corinthians 6:12**

Discussion Questions
1. Why are boundaries important in resisting temptation?
2. What boundaries would help you most in your digital life?
3. What does it mean to experience a spiritual reset, and how can you begin?

Life Application

Choose one boundary this week, such as limiting your screen time to two hours daily or charging your phone outside your bedroom at night.

Action Item

Memorize and share Psalm 51:10: "Create in me a pure heart, O God, and renew a steadfast spirit within me."

Week 6 – Confession and Accountability

Reading Plan: Chapter 7.

Summary:
Addiction thrives in secrecy, but healing begins with confession and accountability. Bringing struggles into the light strips the enemy of power. God calls us to confess our sins and walk with others who will encourage and guide us.

Key Scripture

> "Therefore confess your sins to each other and pray for each other so that you may be healed. The prayer of a righteous person is powerful and effective."
> **James 5:16**

Discussion Questions
1. Why does secrecy make addiction stronger?
2. What makes it hard to confess struggles to God or others?
3. Who can you invite into your life as an accountability partner?

Life Application
Pray this week about who you can trust with your struggles. Take the first step toward confession.

Action Item
Write Psalm 139:23–24 on a card: "Search me, God, and know my heart; test me and know my anxious thoughts. See if there is any offensive way in me, and lead me in the way everlasting." Carry it with you as a reminder.

Week 7 – Renewing the Mind

Reading Plan:
Chapters 8–9 (with special focus on the 40-Day Social Media Freedom Plan).

Summary
The mind is the battlefield. Social media disciples the mind daily with lies of comparison, performance, and idolatry. Renewal comes by filling the mind with God's Word and replacing toxic habits with holy ones. Christ-centered thinking leads to freedom.

Key Scripture

> *"Do not conform to the pattern of this world, but be transformed by the renewing of your mind. Then you will be able to test and approve what God's will is — his good, pleasing and perfect will."*
> **Romans 12:2**

Discussion Questions
1. What lies about yourself or the world have you believed through social media?
2. How can God's Word help you think differently?
3. What step can you take to begin renewing your mind this week?

Life Application
Begin your own 40-Day Social Media Freedom Plan by replacing 15 minutes of screen time with 15 minutes of Bible reading daily.

Action Item

Share Philippians 4:8 with a friend or online: "Finally, brothers and sisters, whatever is true, whatever is noble, whatever is right, whatever is pure, whatever is lovely, whatever is admirable—if anything is excellent or praiseworthy—think about such things."

Week 8 – Restoring Relationships and Living Redeemed

Reading Plan:
Chapters 10–13 and Conclusion.

Summary
Social media promises connection but often delivers loneliness. God calls us to restore authentic relationships in families, churches, and communities. Teens are a chosen generation, called to walk in the light and be set apart for His glory. Redemption is possible through Christ alone.

Key Scripture

> *"But you are a chosen people, a royal priesthood, a holy nation, God's special possession, that you may declare the praises of him who called you out of darkness into his wonderful light."*
> **1 Peter 2:9**

Discussion Questions
1. How has social media hurt your relationships, and how can they be restored?
2. What does it mean to you that you are part of a "chosen generation"?
3. What will you do to live differently after completing this study?

Life Application
Spend intentional time this week with your family or church community — no devices, just fellowship. Share a meal, play a game, or study Scripture together.

Action Item

Pray Joshua 24:15 aloud with your group: "But as for me and my household, we will serve the Lord." Commit together to walk as a redeemed generation.

SMALL GROUP LEADER'S GUIDE

Eight-Week Curriculum for Teens

How to Use This Guide

This Leader's Guide is written to accompany the Teen Participant Guide. Each week follows a consistent structure that helps leaders guide their group through Scripture, reflection, discussion, and life application.

Lesson Flow for Each Week:

1. Opening Prayer & Focus
2. Scripture Reading (always read in full)
3. Lesson Summary & Leader's Notes
4. Life Lesson Story & Biblical Parallel
5. Group Discussion Questions
6. Life Application & Action Step
7. Closing Reflection & Prayer

Tips for Leaders:
1. Encourage honesty without judgment.
2. Protect confidentiality in what is shared.
3. Draw everyone into participation.
4. Keep the group focused on Christ as the source of freedom.

Week 1 – The Darkness Behind the Screen

Focus
Exposing the false light of social media.

Scripture Reading:
1 John 1:5–7

Leader's Notes
Social media promises connection but often delivers comparison, envy, and despair. Light reveals truth, while darkness deceives and enslaves.

Life Lesson Story & Biblical Parallel
Ryan discovered pornography on social media at 13. It altered his view of women, harmed family relationships, and eventually led to devastating consequences. His fall mirrors Amnon's sin against Tamar in 2 Samuel 13 — both cases show how hidden sin destroys lives.

Discussion Questions
1. What kinds of "darkness" hide behind the glow of social media?
2. Why does Scripture describe sin as walking in darkness?
3. How can Christ's light protect us from deception?

Life Application
Track your daily screen time this week and reflect on what portion leads you toward darkness or light.

Closing Prayer
Psalm 119:105

Week 2 – The Seven Deadly Sins in the Digital Age

Focus:
Understanding how sin manifests online.

Scripture Reading:
Romans 6:23

Leader's Notes
Pride, envy, wrath, sloth, greed, lust, and gluttony are magnified by social media. Christ is the antidote, offering humility, contentment, love, diligence, generosity, purity, and self-control.

Life Lesson Stories & Biblical Parallels
Each sin can be illustrated with a teen story (e.g., envy through comparison, wrath through bullying) and a biblical parallel (e.g., Cain and Abel for envy, David and Bathsheba for lust).

Discussion Around the Assessment
This week, have teens complete the Digital Addiction Assessment (from the Participant Guide). Allow 20–25 minutes in small groups for completion and private scoring. Afterward, invite reflection:
1. Which section (behavioral, emotional, relational, spiritual) was highest?
2. Did the results match your expectations?
3. What feelings came up during the assessment?

Leader Guidance
1. Reassure teens that results are not about shame but about awareness.
2. Encourage honesty but never force public sharing.

3. Guide the group to see patterns, addiction thrives in secrecy, but truth sets us free.

Discussion Questions:
1. Which of these sins seems most common online?
2. Why does social media amplify these temptations?
3. How does Christ set us free from them?
4. Life Application: Confess one sin you struggle with and practice the corresponding virtue this week.

Closing Prayer:
　　John 8:36

Week 3 – The Ten Commandments and the Battle for the Soul

Focus:
God's moral law as protection.

Scripture Reading
Exodus 20:1–3

Leader's Notes
The Ten Commandments reveal God's holiness. Social media tempts teens to break each one — idolizing likes, dishonoring parents, coveting what others have, or bearing false witness through gossip.

Life Lesson Story & Biblical Parallels
Examples include Jared dishonoring parents (parallel: Eli's sons), Tasha's sexting scandal (parallel: David & Bathsheba), Emma spreading lies (parallel: false witnesses against Jesus).

Discussion Questions:
1. Which commandment is hardest to keep online?
2. How does God's law protect us rather than restrict us?
3. How can Christ empower us to live holy lives?
4. Life Application: Choose one commandment and live it out online this week.

Closing Prayer:
Psalm 19:14

Week 4 – Addiction, Deviance, and Spiritual Warfare

Focus:
Recognizing addiction and spiritual battle.

Scripture Reading:
Ephesians 6:12

Leader's Notes
Addiction is more than bad habits — it is neurological and spiritual. Dopamine spikes from likes and notifications can enslave the mind. But spiritual warfare is the deeper reality; the devil uses footholds of addiction to gain influence.

Life Lesson Story & Biblical Parallel
Sarah, bullied online, lashed out in rebellion. Only when she discovered the Armor of God did she find strength. Parallel: Jesus resisting temptation in the wilderness (Matthew 4).

Discussion Questions
1. Why is addiction not just psychological but also spiritual?
2. What footholds does the enemy try to gain through social media?
3. How can the Armor of God help us fight back?

Life Application
Teens reflect on one change they want to make based on their assessment and share it with an accountability partner.

Week 5 – Boundaries and Spiritual Reset

Focus:
Establishing protective rhythms.

Scripture Reading:
Romans 12:2

Leader's Notes:
Boundaries guard against bondage; resets renew the soul. Jesus modeled withdrawing to pray. Teens must choose to fast from screens, set device-free times, and reset spiritually.

Life Lesson Story & Biblical Parallel:
The Johnson family's "tech Sabbath" renewed family joy. Parallel: God's gift of Sabbath rest in Exodus 20:8–11.

Discussion Questions:
1. Why do boundaries actually bring freedom?
2. What would a spiritual reset look like for you?
3. How can you reorient your week around Christ?

Life Application
Establish one new boundary this week (e.g., no phones at dinner, screen-free mornings).

Closing Prayer:
Psalm 51:10

Week 6 – Confession and Accountability

Focus:

Freedom through honesty and shared responsibility.

Scripture Reading:

1 John 1:9

Leader's Notes:

Secrecy strengthens sin. Confession exposes it, and accountability sustains freedom. James 5:16 highlights confession and prayer as pathways to healing.

Life Lesson Story & Biblical Parallel:

David battled pornography until he confessed to his pastor, who supported him with prayer and accountability. Parallel: King David's confession after Bathsheba (Psalm 51).

Discussion Questions:

1. Why does confession feel scary but lead to freedom?
2. How does accountability protect us when we are weak?
3. What could accountability look like in your life?
4. Life Application: Teens identify one area for accountability and pray with a trusted partner.

Closing Prayer:

Psalm 139:23–24

Week 7 – Renewing the Mind

Focus:
Filling the mind with God's truth.

Scripture Reading:
Proverbs 23:7a; Philippians 4:8

Leader's Notes:
The mind is the battlefield. Social media fills it with lies; Scripture renews it with truth. Encourage teens to replace scrolling with intentional meditation on God's Word.

Life Lesson Story & Biblical Parallel:
A teen girl reduced anxiety when she began her mornings with Philippians 4:13 instead of Instagram. Parallel: Paul's joy and renewal of mind while imprisoned (Philippians 1).

Discussion Questions:
1. What lies about identity are teens tempted to believe online?
2. How does God's Word reshape the way we think?
3. What steps can you take to walk in the Spirit daily?
4. Life Application: Begin the 40-Day Social Media Freedom Plan.

Closing Prayer:
Philippians 4:8

Week 8 – Restoring Relationships and Living Redeemed

Focus:
Becoming a chosen generation.

Scripture Reading:
1 Peter 2:9; Joshua 24:15

Leader's Notes:
Relationships are God's design for discipleship. Teens are called to live redeemed lives in Christ, set apart from the superficial world of social media.

Life Lesson Story & Biblical Parallel:
A small group of teens fasted from phones during meetings, rediscovering joy and fellowship. Parallel: The early church in Acts 2, devoted to teaching, fellowship, and prayer.

Discussion Questions:
1. How has social media shaped your relationships?
2. What does it mean to live as a chosen generatio≈How can you and your family declare, "We will serve the Lord"?

Life Application
Commit as a group to digital boundaries and Christ-centered practices moving forward.

Closing Prayer:
Joshua 24:15

Small Group Leader's Training

Purpose
To equip small group leaders for sensitive and effective ministry to teens navigating social media addiction.

1. Creating a Safe Environment
- Establish confidentiality: what is shared in the group stays in the group.
- Set expectations for respect: no mocking, no judgment.
- Maintain boundaries: you are a facilitator, not a therapist. Know when to recommend professional help.

2. Handling Sensitive Disclosures
- Listen actively. Don't interrupt.
- Affirm courage in sharing.
- Respond with compassion, not shock.
- Never promise secrecy if abuse or harm is disclosed — follow safeguarding policies.

3. Encouraging Honest Discussion
- Model vulnerability by sharing your own struggles.
- Ask open-ended questions.
- Allow silence — teens sometimes need time to process.
- Draw out quieter voices without pressuring them.

4. Managing Group Flow
- Begin and end with prayer.
- Stay anchored in Scripture, not opinions.
- Watch time carefully so each section is covered.

- Use the Participant Guide as your map but adapt based on group needs.

5. Balancing Grace and Truth
- Extend grace when teens admit failure.
- Speak truth clearly about sin and its consequences.
- Always point back to redemption through Christ.

6. Key Encouragement for Leaders
- You are not alone; rely on the Holy Spirit.
- Your consistency matters more than eloquence.
- Teens will remember your authenticity more than your polish.
- Your role is to plant seeds; God gives the growth (1 Corinthians 3:6–7).

ABOUT THE AUTHOR

Dr. Myron A. Raney, Ph.D., is a Certified Mental Health Advocate, Board-Certified Mental Health Coach, and an active member of the American Association of Christian Counselors. As a Pastoral Counselor and Small Group Leader he is known for his compassionate heart and practical wisdom. He has dedicated his ministry to helping the Church and equipping the next generation to walk in freedom, faith, and hope.

Dr. Raney is also recognized as a leading spirit-filled intellectual thought leader, and Industry Ph.D. specializing in nonprofit management, interdisciplinary social science research, and faith-based community development. With over three decades of experience serving ministry, government, healthcare, and nonprofit organizations, he brings a unique blend of academic rigor and biblical wisdom to his work.

As an emeritus faculty member and the current President and Chairman of Kabalo Research, Inc., Dr. Raney is committed to equipping communities with biblically grounded, research-driven solutions to the challenges of modern life—addressing some of the world's most ominous social problems. He is also a published author, speaker, documentary researcher and film maker, and advocates for youth and families navigating the pressures of today's digital culture.

ABOUT THE AUTHOR

Author Contact
Phone – (800) 476-2184
Email – contact@kabalo.cc
www.kabalo.cc

www.ingramcontent.com/pod-product-compliance
Lightning Source LLC
Chambersburg PA
CBHW050336010526
44119CB00037B/464/J